Endorsements

"In a world of texts, emails, and one-day delivery on anything we want, it's tempting to expect the same speed and resolution in relationships. But meaningful marriages, workplace alliances, or healthy neighbor connections require extended time and a process for effectively sharing life together. **Stay in the Room** is the guidebook for the authenticity and transparency that lead to redemptive, reconciled, and restorative relationships desired for living fully alive."

—Dan Miller, author of *48 Days to the Work You Love*, and host of the "48 Days Podcast"

"We have many books on relationships today. Most are by people who have merely read other books. Dan Francis is different. He has known tragedy. He has battled for his own wholeness. He has studied and invested to see others made whole too. He is now a skilled guide for the relationships we all dream of having. Believe me, you want this book!"

—Stephen Mansfield, PhD
New York Times Bestselling Author

STAY IN
THE ROOM

Transform your troubled relationships

DAN FRANCIS, PH.D.

FREILING
PUBLISHING

Published by Freiling Publishing, a division of Freiling Agency, LLC.

P.O. Box 1264,
Warrenton, VA 20188

www.FreilingPublishing.com

ISBN 978-1-950948-67-3

Printed in the United States of America

Contents

Acknowledgments

IN HIS MEMOIR on writing, Stephen King said, "Writing is a lonely job. Having someone who believes in you makes a lot of difference. They don't have to make speeches. Just believing is usually enough."

Dr. George Buttrick, my professor and mentor, commented in red on an assignment: "You have a gift for words. Do not take this for granted or use it for yourself." The words created a freeze frame moment in my life. They spurred me on, for ultimately, I longed to communicate with clarity and hope about life changing matters.

Fast forward a few decades. I passed around a first draft of this book to my accountability guys, called the Tuesday Group. A fiancé of one friend, Cynthia Greer, borrowed a copy and responded, "If you don't publish it, I will!" Her freeze framing words helped me surge on.

Everyone needs a PERSON. We need the ONE whose believing makes not simply A difference, but THE difference. It helps immensely when the difference maker in your life and labor is your bride of 43 years. My Neva offers an unusual mix of unconditional love and unashamed honesty. Each word on every page survived her loving laser. My heart is full.

A final word about the two from my ONE. Nicholas, our first born, and Christen, the mother of our two grandchildren, have not only grown up in my *room*, but have *stayed* beyond their duty to Dad. They remain the delight of my life.

Stay in the Room Relationships

"The two most important days in your life, the day you are born, and
the day you figure out why."[1]

Mark Twain

Introduction

A KENTUCKY STATE POLICE officer intrudes the playground of two
brothers, six and eight years old, frolicking in the front room of
an old house. He seeks entrance to a door rarely opened leading into a
room stacked with unused furniture. Like many homes, the driveway
and arrival destination reverse the original entrance to the house.

My brother and I are frightened, wondering who reported us to
the police. We suspect the officer is there to assess the damage done
to the upside-down end tables acting as sleds for our rambunctious
imaginations.

The officer's question, "Is your mother home?" forever changes the
texture and taste of the word family. From a simple and tender understanding of belonging, my family is now broken and aching.

A brief conversation brings tears to Mom's eyes and so begins my first
memory of relational pain . . . the pain born of a dad who is electrocuted
climbing down from a power pole on a Friday afternoon in 1958. My
mother's tears become a river, flowing into decades of relational pain.

That day and the days to follow fill me with an incessant need to run.

Fast forward thirteen years, "Brother Turner, I just want you to
know, Sandy and I are breaking up and I need for you to pray for us." A
simple statement of reality is the beginning of the end of boy meets girl,
falls in love, thus extinguishing their happily ever after.

A three-and-a-half-year relationship is over, amid tears and disappointment. Most likely to succeed, with a hope chest of anticipation, we go in different directions. Years of high school romance, filled with proms and homecoming queen celebrations, are over. The pit in my stomach lingers as reality forces me to face the future, disillusioned.

That day and the days to follow fill me with an incessant need to run.

Fast forward twelve years. A young pastor, two years out of seminary, sits at a lunch table with a prominent businessman and well-known leader in the church who says, "I think your ministry is going to fail." This cruel and intimidating statement is the beginning of my belief that church folk are always nice and play fair.

The words hit like bullets, tearing the trajectory of my life, present and future. My body freeze-frames the words as my heart beats thunderously in my chest. I listen, hoping to catch my breath and have the oxygen to form words out of my whirling emotions. All I can say is, "I am sorry you feel that way."

That day and the days to follow fill me with an incessant need to run.

THE RELATIONAL RUN

You get the idea. Relational work is heavy and harsh. Fraught with pain and misunderstanding, the most natural, but regretful response to the workload of relationships is to run. The only problem is relationships are also exhilarating and essential.

For as long as I can remember, I have marveled at the mystery of relationships. The product of a relationally dysfunctional home, my journey screams like the plea from Rodney King after the 1992 Los Angeles riots: "Can we all get along?"[2]

At age six, my father passes and my mother spirals through grief with three children below the age of eight. Her parents, already divorced and distant, supply no assistance. Her slide toward a concoction of vodka and tomato juice, aptly called a Bloody Mary, becomes her soothing solace in the night. Men soon enter her world, more as providers and protectors than lovers and husbands. She marries again and again and again, the final one, younger than me.

With husbands come other siblings, three to be exact, and the relational dysfunction, birthed by grief, now explodes with competing bloodlines and pecking orders. Stir this with the sickness of two alcoholic stepfathers, and we have relational dysfunction on steroids.

My first hint of safety from this relational chasm comes at school. A caring third grade teacher by the name of (you are not going to believe this!) Mrs. Francis nurtures me toward excellence. I find my self-esteem in books and academic achievement which translates into my first taste of relational confidence.

During high school, my trend to escape the madness of home life with academic achievement and personal popularity continues. A screaming symbol of my need to belong and obtain value is realized when voted Best Dressed in my senior class of almost 400 students.

It's the spring of 1970 and I want to wallow in my high school successes. Life is good. Then once again, reality comes knocking with a series of events that forever change me. I am called to the school office. An odd request, the school officials tell me to leave school and go by the home of longtime family friend and fellow rock band member, Gary Schoberg. Knowing he is a Sergeant in the Army, fighting a war in Vietnam, I brace for the worst. I had played many a drum roll with Gary, but none so strong as my heartbeat that day.

An American flag in front of the house, waving at half-mast, brings a gasp to my chest. Heart pounding, I knock on the door and find the devastated face of Gary's weeping mother. No words are needed. Her son, my friend, dies in Vietnam, only a few weeks from coming home.

I want to run.

Despite the grief of those weeks, the beginning of the summer is filled with celebration and anticipation. My high school friends and I graduate into young adulthood, seeking the spoils of our newly acquired choices and chances. Within weeks, one of those choices and chances becomes deadly. Four of my high school drinking buddies are driving home after a day of revelry when suddenly, the car flips, killing one of the most popular guys in our senior class, Mark Spencer. The friend we call Spence is gone.

I want to run.

Only a few weeks before leaving for college life on the big campus, my two closest friends visit me at different times with similar stories. Kevin was president of my senior class. I presented his nomination speech. He is a fellow drinking buddy, and weekend partier. He knocks on my door to share his experience at a Christian retreat. He asks if I have ever thought about accepting Jesus Christ as my Savior. Respectful of his newfound joy, but not comprehending the gravity of his question, I deflect the offer to make a decision.

Within days, my long-time trophy, prom-queen, homecoming queen, and cheerleader girlfriend, offers similar advice. She uses a new word about our relationship. She says it is carnal, and after going to a Christian retreat (yes, another one of those), she suggests some distance to sort things out.

I want to run.

A concert date had been on the calendar all summer, so we agree, going to the Three Dog Night concert in Louisville, Kentucky, is still on. Four couples, in two cars, we begin our journey for a night of music and merriment. Anticipating a need to impress my now crazy-talking girlfriend, I do what any hot-blooded eighteen–year-old male would do in the 70s. I put chrome mag-wheels on my car. Oh, the misguided web we males weave in the name of love and lust. I suspect she never even noticed!

Riding down the expressway, I suddenly feel the need to pull over. For the life of me, I cannot remember if it was a restroom break or simply a divine urging, but I motion to the other car, and we glide up the exit ramp. I apply the brakes and almost simultaneously, the car stops and drops. The front right side of my midnight black, 1969 Pontiac Grand Prix, suddenly rests on the ground.

With a mixture of fear and relief, I get out of the car. Standing in a light drizzling rain, I see the new mag wheel lying on the ground. By the wheel well of the car, all five studs (those things that hold the wheel and tire on the car) are broken. As I stare, attempting to grasp what I see, I hear a voice. Yes, call me schizophrenic, call me delusional, but clearly call me confident. I hear a voice say, "I love you this much!"

I want to run.

A PLEA TO STAY IN THE ROOM

Common to each of these circumstances and encounters with both human and divine relationships is a desire to run. Misunderstanding, confusion, anger, and mystery are gasoline in the tank of relational runaways. Pain and disappointment can either be our companion on the run, or the GPS that steers us to a rest stop for re-routing.

If my life experience is the norm, most people NEVER stop running from relationships. We deflect, defer or defend our way through the relational debris of life. We jog in unhealthy circles of blame and brokenness, unwilling to accept responsibility to stay in the room with difficult relationships.

Without fully realizing it through the years, I begin using the phrase "stay in the room" to characterize the single most important ingredient for every significant relationship. Every relationship goes through disagreements and confrontations resulting in retreat out of fear, hurt, vengeance and blame. The image on page 8 reflects a visual of this understanding.

The issue is not IF we encounter these moments of conflict, but WHEN and HOW we assess our relational differences within a context of proximity.

Will we choose to stay in proximity to the problem or simply run? I determined that I must learn to stay in the room rather than run. We must learn to agree to disagree without discounting the other person. We must learn to compromise without holding a grudge. We must learn to replace getting even with getting together. We must learn to trade fear for respect. We must learn to hold onto hurt only long enough to refine and facilitate healing.

So, what qualifies me to speak to this concept of **Stay in the Room** relationships? First, I have survived and even thrived, despite the dysfunctional onslaught of growing up in a destructive and divided home. Second, I have experienced four decades of a crazy-happy marriage which has undergirded my ability to speak and teach to thousands of people through my years as a minister.

OVERVIEW: A RELATIONAL CANON

It comes from an odd source with a long title. George L. Hersey's book, *The Evolution of Allure: Sexual Selection From the Medici Venus to the Incredible Hulk,* concludes that if there is an ideal form for the human body, it is the Ironman.[3]

For the uninitiated, Ironman refers to an athlete who competes in a grueling triathlon of swimming, bicycling and running. Designed to push the human body to its limits, the Ironman or Iron Woman is generally recognized as Hersey concludes, the body canon or ideal form for the human body.

The most decorated Ironman is Mark Allen, who is now retired, but his list of accomplishments includes being the six-time Ironman winner and holder of the title The World's Fittest Man. He has devised a 16-week program for ultimate fitness.[4] He believes if we follow his complete training regime for five hours a week, we will be startled at the results. Even stranger, Allen calls the training regime a meditation for the entire body.

To be an Ironman athlete, Mark Allen divides his training into four components. These include . . .

heart training for endurance;

mind training for attitude;

nutritional training for internal fitness; and

strength training for muscle mass.

I find a powerful parallel between these physical categories for a body canon, and the spiritual and emotional categories for a relational canon.

Being a student of the Bible, I am drawn to Allen's components for ultimate fitness. They easily fall into the categories offered in Judaism's most sacred prayer, the *Shema,* (Deuteronomy 6:4-6) as well as Jesus' use of those verses to answer the greatest commandment question in Mark 12:28-30:

"Hear, O Israel! The Lord is our God, the Lord is one! You shall love the Lord your God with all your *heart* and with all your *soul* and with all your *might* (power*)*. These words, which I am commanding you today, shall be on your heart" (Deuteronomy 6:4-6 **NAS**).

"One of the scribes came and heard them arguing, and recognizing that He had answered them well, asked Him, 'What commandment is the foremost of all?' Jesus answered, 'The foremost is, Hear, O Israel! The Lord our God is one Lord; and you shall love the Lord your God with all your **heart**, and with all your **soul**, and with all your **mind**, and with all your **strength**'" (Mark 12:28, **NAS**).

A closer look at the original Greek words present in the different passages using some portion of the *Shema* in the Bible uncovers five different words: *Kardia* (heart), *Psyche* (soul), *Dunamis* (power), *Dianoia* (mind) and *Ischus* (strength).

While divisions for this book were identified before I made the connection to Allen's body canon and the *Shema*, my sense of balance is rewarded when I discover the fifth word and category for compatibility. The fifth word is *Dunamis* or power and is more than suitable for my understanding of compatibility.

Let's examine five categories for relational health and wholeness.

AUTHENTICITY: SOUL TRAINING FOR TRANSPARENCY

As with every good exercise system, Mark Allen includes a nutritional plan, but instead of advocating a sports drink or diet plan, he suggests we stop and listen to our bodies. The body will communicate what it needs.

Likewise, when we desire healthy relationships, we must establish a relationship regime that includes authenticity, or soul training for transparency. Just as we listen to our physical body for nutritional insight, we must listen to our inner being, or soul, if we desire the opportunity to be authentic in our relationships.

BOUNDARIES: STRENGTH TRAINING FOR DECISION-MAKING

Mark Allen, and other triathletes explain the point of strength training is not to get larger muscles, but better muscles. The goal for triathletes is enduring performance, not bulk.

Similarly, those desiring to strengthen their relational health must draw careful and accommodating boundaries. The only task more difficult than setting a healthy relational boundary is re-establishing old, tired, unsuccessful boundaries. We must learn the power of an appropriate "no" as well as the necessity of a strategic "yes."

COMPATIBILITY: RELATIONAL TRAINING FOR VULNERABILITY

The issue of compatibility does not fit neatly within the other four categories. A look at the origin of my categories will help explain.

After several decades of counseling and mentoring people with relational difficulties, I developed a list of issues, which parallels my own relational battles. From that list, five categories of relational needs surface and for quick retrieval, I place them in an easy-to-remember acrostic, A-E alphabetically. Over time, I formulate what you see in this book.

In shaping the four themes, I realize, while compatibility does not fit perfectly within the other categories, it certainly fits our overall theme, so I place it in the middle. Compatibility, by its nature, is a core ingredient for relational health because it neither feeds on nor runs from conflict. Compatibility is the door to the room of every relationship. Compatibility is the key if we desire **Stay in the Room** perseverance as both a goal and a grace to loving vulnerability.

DISCERNMENT: MIND TRAINING FOR PERSPECTIVE

An Ironman and Iron Woman race course is daunting. It usually exists of a 2.4-mile swim, a 112-mile bike ride and a marathon run of

26.2 miles. Just thinking about it can shake your confidence. Allen's training recognizes the power of attitude and its importance in finishing the race.

Discernment is the mind-muscle, which must be developed if we hope to live in healthy, whole relationships. For the follower of Christ, a mind trained in the things of God will battle selfishness and hurt and focus on offering each person the benefit of doubt.

ENTHUSIASM: HEART TRAINING FOR ENDURANCE

Mark Allen urges his athletes to train slowly, easily, and with patience. "Go for long-term gain, not immediate gratification,"[5] says Allen. Building endurance and stamina depends on steady, incremental gains, not flurries of heart-beating exercises followed by weeks of inactivity.

Experienced triathletes describe how staying below the aerobic threshold will chew up fat reserves needed for fuel instead of the day's carbohydrate intake. Our aerobic threshold is that point where our bodies stop consuming fat and dip into muscle, which explains why many runners are so thin and appear emaciated. "Your body has up to 50 times more energy dammed up in its fat stores than the measly 2,000 carbohydrate calories that can be stored as glycogen,"[6] Allen concludes.

Being able to love God and others with **Stay in the Room** relationships involves a steady stream of dedication and perseverance. Too often our crowded lives produce a hurried stance of discouragement and emptiness. Too busy to soak our lives in the fuel of God's strength through prayer, Bible study, and relational accountability, we exist on leftover resources and weakened aspirations. Honestly, without strength and endurance, the race we run will be unfinished and unfulfilling.

The next five chapters will examine these five categories and develop strategies for living **Stay in the Room** relationships.

1

"Authenticity: Can I really tell you who I am?"

AUTHENTICITY: SOUL TRAINING FOR TRANSPARENCY

"Be who you are and say what you feel because those who mind don't matter and those who matter don't mind."[7]

Bernard M. Baruch

THE HOUSE IS on a dead-end street. While the location is ideal for a nine-year-old boy to ride his bike and shoot his BB gun, the reason for living there is freshly awkward. "He's your new dad, or step-dad," Mom explains to the three of us. A new house means a new school with different friends and teachers. It also brings a fearful pit in my stomach on the first day of school. When I am uneasy about the man who lives in my home, how can I be secure about new faces at school?

My fear is fully realized. I walk into the third-grade classroom and my teacher is a cross between the She-Wolf of London and Frankenstein's daughter. Really. She glares at the new kid and points unceremoniously to my seat. Days go by without incident, and just when I feel safe, I walk to her desk during a work time to ask a question. The glare is back, and this time she follows it with a swipe and a shove. The book flies out of my hands and before it even lands, she orders me to stand in the corner. I face the wall, feeling the wide-eyed stares of every child in the room.

The recess bell rings, shattering the tension in the room. Wondering what to do, she signals me to join the other children. My body breaks free from the frozen stance and I walk slowly toward the door, then to the playground, then to my home. That is correct. Once I get to the playground, watching the other children play, I sneak out the side of the playground nearest my new home.

I want to run, so I do.

I run the two blocks to my house and fortunately, find it empty. Mom is out so I quickly search for a hiding place. Not overly creative, I find a closet and make my way behind the clothes. In moments, the front door opens, and as if she has a built-in GPS, Mom walks to the closet and discovers my feet extending below the hanging clothes. A very short discussion ensues. My nine-year-old mind remembers it going some-thing like this: "What in the hell are you doing home?" "I don't like my teacher so I came home." "Well, I don't like lots of things, but that doesn't mean you come home and run from your problems." She then abruptly informs me we will return to school.

It is an outrageous understatement to say my Mom was no pushover. She would later ride a motorcycle, drive powder-puff race cars and carry a .38 revolver in her purse for protection.

Steeled from her battle with grief and single-mom responsibilities, she marches me into the school and demands to see the principal. Sitting outside the office, I hear words like "we don't move children into other classrooms" and "oh, yes you will!" Like a roaring mother bear shouting fear into an approaching mountain lion, she wins the tug-of-war of wills and the principal escorts me to my new class. There I met my new teacher, Mrs. Francis, my angel from heaven who literally changed my life. I could have never imagined that some forty years later, I would become her minister and friend and was honored to offer comfort during her final moments and speak at her funeral on February 9, 2018.

From the moment of our first social embarrassment, we become painfully aware of the judgment and rejection of people. Whether nine years old or ninety, rejection is always crushing. Rejection pulls and prods us either to acquiesce to the expectations of others or to rise above them and claim a different and likely, lonely path. It is in this rising above that we become acquainted with the bedrock value of authenticity.

Authenticity is the ability and willingness to tell who you are, and it is birthed in relational risk. According to the dictionary, something is authentic when it conforms to fact or reality and is genuine. Yes, there can be different perspectives of reality. Those committed to authenticity care less about their perspective and more about arriving at a mutual understanding of what is real and genuine for the health of their relationship.

Who doesn't want to connect relationally with someone willing to be honest and forthright? On the flip side, who wants to invest emotional energy into a relationship fraught with dishonesty and superficiality?

Jesus speaks of authenticity in a broad sense when he says "I came into the world to bring everything into the clear light of day, making all distinctions clear; so that those who have never seen will see, and those who have made a great pretense of seeing will be exposed as blind" (John 9: 39, *The Message*). The thought, life, and plan that Jesus introduces has authenticity at the core.

Assuming authenticity is vital, why do we struggle to offer and receive it?

WHAT KEEPS US FROM BEING AUTHENTIC?

■ Sin

Even if you do not have an understanding of sin as identified within the Judeo-Christian tradition, most understand the concept of right and wrong. We are right when we value others and ourselves and wrong when we do not. Keith Miller defines sin as "the universal and self-defeating interior bent toward a powerful, rebellious self-centeredness."[8]

For a follower of Christ, sin is the starting point for understanding our inclination toward relational dishonesty. Sin is the distortion of who and what God, the Creator, designs for us, the created. Sin is the part of us that clings to self-centeredness and manipulation. If we believe in

God as our Creator, our role as the created needs a relationship not only with God, but also with other created beings in order to be genuine and authentic.

If we do not have a belief in God as Creator for our starting point, often our sense of justice and belief in right and wrong will lead to an ethic of fairness that identifies our need for authenticity. No matter how we arrive, most agree the starting point and overarching theme for vibrant relationships is authenticity. We must know and trust ourselves well enough to answer absolutely to the question, can I tell you who I am?

Cecil T. Turner is not able to do this. An Associated Press story tells the sad tale of this fifty-year-old in Louisville, Kentucky, who is convicted of slipping into at least three churches, stealing money and a credit card. What is bizarre about Turner's case is how he is caught: using the stolen credit card to buy merchandise from Christian bookstores. The thief purchases ten copies of a Bible study called *Making Peace With Your Past*, as well as a follow-up study, *Moving Beyond Your Past*.[9] The inauthentic nature of his decisions are both comedic and sad.

Call it whatever you desire, but clearly there is a deficiency in the human heart that needs to be identified, and for those who profess a faith in God, that starts with an acknowledgement of sin.

■ Satan

Evil is a deep, frustrating, mysterious force that is part of the fabric of individual and social life. The experience of this invisible counterforce is so personal, the Bible gives it a name—Satan. Keith Miller defines Satan as "the adversarial force, exerting strong energy—either very subtly or violently—to influence our lives, inside and out, 'away from' the search for reality, unselfish love, and God."[10]

If we do not believe in sin or Satan, we usually blame bad behavior on circumstances outside our control (abusive parents, uncaring governments or unfortunate marriages). With each step toward personal and relational growth, we can either deny responsibility or blame some *one* or some *thing*, or we can accept responsibility and be accountable in all our relationships. My plea is for a relational accountability that accepts the need for authenticity in ALL relationships.

Jayson Blair was a star *New York Times* reporter until he was charged with plagiarism and the faking of reports. In a review of his book, *Burning Down My Master's House: My Life at the New York Times,* Jack Shafer writes the following: "Because Blair spends most of *Burning Down My Master's House* reclining on the shrink's couch seeking our sympathy, it's fair to psychoanalyze him from afar. Citing this shoddily written and filibustering book as evidence, one could argue that Blair barely had the talent to work as a cub reporter on a small-town daily, let alone a major newspaper. Those who can't, steal and fabricate. The best explanation of why he lies and continues to dissemble is also provided in this book: he seems most alive in the book when he's walking the ethical tightrope and hoodwinking somebody. Every con man loves his con, and few are as lucky as Blair to enshrine their version in book form."[11]

Whether our understanding of evil has a name or is simply an inclination in our heart to duplicity, authenticity will demand cold and calculated ownership of our choices, their costs and consequences.

■ Self/Soul

Soviet dissident, writer and winner of the 1970 Nobel Prize in Literature, Alexander Solzhenitsyn says, "The meaning of earthly existence is not, as we have grown used to thinking, in prosperity, but in the development of the soul."[12] The meaning of existence is to preserve unspoiled, undisturbed and undistorted the image of eternity born in each person.

While sin and Satan are real causal factors in our inability to discover and experience authenticity, it is the lack of the development of a soul that ultimately leads to the death of authenticity in our relationships.

While the word "soul" differs in definition depending on each person's background and starting point, a general definition is as follows: a soul is the moral or emotional nature of a human being. Most of us interact with an internal part of us that is both moral and emotional and the development and understanding of this, the soul, is crucial to being true to ourselves.

Some of us call this internal part our self. Whatever we call this internal conversation and moral consciousness, the self plays a leading role in our search for authenticity. It is the search for the answer to the two-fold question: "Do I know who I am?" and "Can I really tell you who I am?"

HOW DO WE SHAPE OUR SOUL/SELF FOR AUTHENTICITY?

Our ability to be authentic is determined by the shape of our soul or the self. As a follower of Christ, my search for the answer to the above question forces me to evaluate this in context of scripture. There are more than 240 references to the word soul in the Bible with four different meanings:

The Bible says the soul is the internal part of us . . .

• where our deepest *feelings* and *desires* reside.

"O God, look at the trouble I'm in! My stomach in knots, my heart wrecked by a life of rebellion" (Lam. 1:20, *The Message*).

• where our personality relates to **God.**

Jesus said, "That you love the Lord your God with all your passion and prayer and muscle and intelligence" (Luke 10: 27, *The Message*).

• where our highest *values* are processed.

Then Jesus went to work on his disciples. "Anyone who intends to come with me has to let me lead. You're not in the driver's seat; I am. Don't run from suffering; embrace it. Follow me and I'll show you how. Self-help is no help at all. Self-sacrifice is the way, my way, to finding yourself, your true self. What kind of deal is it to get everything you want but lose yourself? What could you ever trade your soul for?" (Matthew 16:24-26, *The Message*).

• that will continue after *life.*

"When he ripped off the fifth seal, I saw the souls of those killed because they had held firm in their witness to the Word of God. They were gathered under the Altar and cried out in loud prayers" (Revelation 6:9, *The Message*).

Keith Miller personalizes his view of the soul as "the potential hero of the imperfect cast of an individual's spiritual drama."[13] So, with this understanding of the soul, how does our soul act as the potential champion of our lives and our quest for authenticity? It does so in at least two ways.

The soul acts as a measuring stick. It acts as a personal guide and advisor as we live our spiritual drama. The soul is that distinctive part of us reflecting and drawing us to what is uniquely us. In its purest form, the soul prompts us toward honesty and integrity. It is not surprising for those who see God as the ultimate reality; the soul is the personality's contact point with God and spearheads any hope for authenticity.

The soul also acts as a whistle-blower. The Psalmist declares: "My soul is starved and hungry, ravenous! —insatiable for your nourishing commands" (Psalm 119:20, *The Message*). The writer says there is something from within calling us to our highest values. It is a gnawing, nudging reminder to be better and do more in our quest for relational authenticity.

When I speak about the role of the soul in authenticity, I sometimes use a hula-hoop. For the uninformed, a hula-hoop is a toy often misunderstood as being invented in the 1950s, although it has existed for thousands of years. It is a small, often colorful circular plastic tube that is twirled around the waist, limbs or neck. Originally, the ancient Greeks swung a hoop around their waist for physical fitness.

For demonstration purposes, I place the hula-hoop on the floor and stand inside it. I describe how being in sync with God allows me to be authentic with both God and people. Then standing outside of the hoop, I demonstrate that being out of sync with my soul forces me to listen more to the imperfect cast of characters sprinkling my experience with life-draining moments, causing me to stray from the soul-sync or alignment I desperately need for authenticity.

WHAT ARE THE GUIDING HUNGERS
SHAPING OUR SOUL/SELF?

Meet my one and only granddaughter, Jensen Everleigh Endicott. It is with loving fascination that I watch her journey from unconsciousness to consciousness, to self-consciousness, to self-centeredness, and then to some degree, back and forth again. With each step comes newfound freedoms and parallel challenges. I marvel at the internal guidance system (IGS) composed of longings and hungers nudging Jensen beyond herself in spite of her fears and search for self-esteem.

It begins early with Jensen. She becomes our entertainer. Her first smiles transition into exuberant joy. From a winning grin to a contagious smile, she ultimately develops this over-the-top exaltation of ecstasy where she stiffens her legs, lifts her hands and gleefully inhales and exhales with machine-gun-type staccato, face fixated on expressing utter joy. Our laughter only extends her exclamations.

Not long after this, her mother trains her to respond to words even before she fully comprehends. Our daughter, Christen, would say the word "boys" and Jensen, on cue, would quickly put her hand in front of her as if she was blocking someone from getting close to her and say, "Ew!" Over and over again, she would entertain us with her comical response to the word, "boys."

Then came her desire (due to my wife Neva's encouragement) to sing the familiar baseball song, "Take me out to the Ballgame" as well as the nursery rhyme, "Jack and Jill went up the hill." She recites them with such expression and delight that she regularly performs them for others. Not surprisingly, we have them recorded for future viewing and priceless memories.

As an eleven-year-old, Jensen's outward expressions of joy include dancing and singing. My reason for mentioning this is simply to remind us of the journey and development of the soul, that internal guidance system that leads us to find satisfiers for our specific needs. Jensen learned early and often how to satisfy her audience and her self-esteem grew with each encounter. Her ability and risk were rewarded. Make careful note of this.

Finding healthy, appropriate satisfiers for our specific wants and needs directly impacts the answer to the question: "Can I really tell you who I am?"

Richard Grant and Andrea Wells Miller, in *Recovering Connections*, identify four guiding longings or hungers that impact the "shaping of our soul."[14]

- **The hunger for *parents*.** (birth to 18 months)

This is the "hold me" stage. Due to the separation trauma at birth, the need to form a bond with dependable adults is crucial to the growth and well-being of a newborn. This yearning for dependence lays an important foundation for social, and spiritual experiences later in life.

It would be impossible to know the value of the person in a child's life that fosters all the unhurried moments . . . those spent snuggling on a couch, in a rocker, or at a bedside for evening prayers. It is a warm, comforting place. It is a treasured place. It is a safe place for the thousands of curiosities that arise about God, friendship and all the "what if" questions. It is a place where trust is learned, tested and practiced. It is a place where moral fibers of the future are formed.

- **The hunger for *companionship*.** (18 months to 4 years)

This is the "who are you" stage. It is the nudging toward other people both in and outside the family.

The importance of modeling is critical during this stage of language development, potty training, and the safety of risk during new tasks. Learning to navigate what is MINE and the decisions of when to share are made here. The need for safety and belonging is growing. The acceptance or rejection of this hunger either calms or awakens feelings of fear or security.

- **The hunger for *power* and *freedom*.** (4 years to 6 years)

This is the classic "I can do it myself" stage. Whether it is choosing to make a friend, tie a shoe, or try hard at school, these individual power blocks build a personality.

Most children in this age bracket are experiencing life in groups; i.e. nursery school and first grade. They hopefully build confidence in learning nursery rhymes, songs and the alphabet. They begin to want screen time. Some have first experiences on a sports team of T-ball, gymnastics or soccer. Self-esteem is built as they exert personal power, authority, freedom and boundaries.

- **The hunger for *meaning*.** (6 years to puberty)

This is the "So, what is life all about?" stage. The yearning for meaning seeks a design or explanation for coalescing the experiences and knowledge gathered to this point. What we learn if we continue to pursue this hunger is how an intimate relationship does not come through academic pursuits, but through caring contact.

It is not an exaggeration to say our inability to satisfy these hungers exacerbates some level of fear and shame, which can produce a lack of self-confidence and self-esteem. This battle within the soul has been appropriately called "the dark night of the soul."

Bottom line: No one relishes or plans on being phony. The good news is that no one needs to be; the authentic life is the only road to a clear conscience and a peaceful heart.

A WAY TO LOOK AT AUTHENTICITY

As a reader of the popular magazine, *Fast Company*, I am drawn to an article by Bill Breen entitled, "Who do you love?"[15] The writer discusses the issue of authenticity and identifies a fourfold approach to the word's origin. He says authenticity comes from a sense of place, a larger purpose, a strong point of view and integrity.

While he applies these ideas to consumer products, I am drawn to his definition of the qualities of authenticity and how they can apply to authentic relationships.

Sense of Place . . . Identify where you are

Breen uses a sense of place as an ingredient for authenticity in branding products, but I think of the identity issue in the context of relationships. Whether you desire a relationship with another person in business or romance, the identity question, which asks, "where are you (we)" is paramount and primary.

Every relationship should have a Global Positioning System (GPS) for navigation, which forces us to identify two key ingredients of every journey: starting point (how did we meet?) and destination (where does this relationship need to go?). Do these seem a bit technical or laborious? The answer will depend on how many of your relationships go salty and south because one or both parties confuse or change the key elements of the starting point and destination.

Monitoring where we are in key and influential relationships is crucial to creating and maintaining authenticity. An influential relationship is simply a relationship where what we do influences the other person and what they do influences us. If each person has different starting points and destinations for the relationship, the potential for authenticity decreases dramatically.

■ A "Sense of Place" story . . .

Sandy, my three-year girlfriend and faith partner, is two years behind me in her journey from high school to college. At age 18, I experience a conversion to faith in Christ and within a year, commit my life to full-time ministry. I come home from the University of Kentucky to finish college at Northern Kentucky University as Sandy is stepping into the whirlwind journey from high school to college campus. The geographical distance creates more relational distance than our life plans can sustain.

While the breakup is mutual in its finality, the last few months leading to the decision are saturated with sadness over broken promises and fears of unexpected loneliness. As Sandy moves toward other experiences, I find myself moving away from attachments, in particular, relationships. Experiencing relational hurt for the first time, I move into a stage with the opposite sex I call my Monk Stage. For the first time since Marjeanie Applegate, my first girlfriend in middle school, I do not have a formal girlfriend.

Do you suspect my childhood trauma has anything to do with my need to belong to a girlfriend in a recognized relationship? No wonder, over the next twelve to eighteen months, I basically choose to be alone. My identity is in turmoil and other companions only confuse the rebuilding process. How can I be authentic and tell you who I am, if I either do not know or I do not know outside of connection with another person in a recognized relationship?

What I learned in my Monk Stage and relearned through many years of observing and encouraging relational maturity is no earthly relationship can bring the soul satisfaction birthed in a life-transforming encounter with God. Earthly relationships can encourage and support it, but they cannot replace it. This is where so many romantic relationships go wrong.

Authenticity about where we are in any relationship is the oxygen that breathes honesty and life into all our relationships. Having a sense of place is crucial to understanding and being an authentic, honest person. However, our world does not always encourage that kind of transparency.

■ A Sense of Place travesty . . .

Are you aware of the wizardry in cell phone technology that allows a person to program a cell phone to ring at just the right moment?

A few years ago, Cingular Wireless and Virgin Mobile cell phone companies began offering Escape-A-Date,[16] a rescue service for those in awkward situations. Imagine the unbearable silence broken by an urgent call summoning you to leave immediately. A programmed cell phone calls to provide an excuse for a person wanting to leave an unpleasant situation.

Both companies offer scripts designed for urgent rescue such as a heart attack or car wreck of a loved one. The company describes the rescue service as a lifestyle accessory for modern people who want their phone to serve them. Who wants an uncomfortable situation any longer than absolutely necessary? By one estimate at least ten thousand calls a month have been generated by fake rescue call services.

This parallels a service offered by a company where ATM-itations (fake receipts) come 24 to a pack for $3.99. These include the bank name of Fidelity National Bank & Savings (FNBS) with a withdrawal amount of $400 and a balance of $314,159.26. The BS in the bank's acronym should be a dead giveaway. If not, take a close look at the balance. It is the first eight numbers of pi, as in pie in your face.[17]

Honestly, what does it say about our world if we require the services of communication networks and fake bank receipts to maneuver our social interactions? Are we so lacking in social and communication skills that our authenticity cannot carry the load of honest interchange?

Larger Purpose . . . Identify what and who you will be

Breen uses larger purpose as the second ingredient for authenticity in the consumer market. In the context of our discussion on relationships, this larger purpose seeks to find relational authenticity by asking the question, "what (is this relationship) and who will I be" as a result of this relationship? These two questions seek to identify the larger purpose of each of our relationships within the context of authenticity.

While the previous "who are you" question speaks to the starting point of pursuing authentic relationships, the "what and who you will be" question relates to the expected destination step.

In the film, *Catch Me If You Can*, Leonardo DiCaprio plays a man who bluffs his way through nearly a dozen professions, including airline pilot, physician and banker, before being discovered. The film is based on the true story of a young man who cons his way through life, making millions. He is so skilled at faking his identity that after capture he is employed to uncover other frauds by the FBI.

Let me also introduce you to Father Frederico B. Gomez de Esparza. Father "Fred" was a Catholic priest from Mexico who served bilingual parishes in Arizona several years ago. By all accounts, Father Fred did his job well. "Everybody loved him, (and) thought he was a great priest. He's great, gave a great homily . . ." says Maria Doten, a parishioner at Immaculate Conception Parish in Yuma, Arizona. Even his superiors agreed. According to Monsignor Richard O'Keefe, "He had a great knowledge of the workings of the church, great knowledge of the history of the church. He knew the Scriptures and he was able to come up with some very good answers."[18]

Like other clergy, Father Fred administered the sacraments, comforted the sick, preached and conducted weddings and funerals. He did everything clergy are expected to do. However, Father Frederico was actually Fred Brita, disguised as Dr. Mark Esparza (a court-appointed psychiatrist), Mark Gomez (community activist), and Frederi DiBritto (fundraiser for the UCLA Medical School).

After five criminal convictions while in his 20s, he believed no one would hire an ex-con. Brito decided to morph himself into positions of trust and responsibility. Being very astute, he spent enough time in a courtroom to mimic a court-appointed psychiatrist and took enough seminary courses to know the basics of being a clergyman. Staying one step ahead of the authorities, Brito figured the FBI would not think to look for him in a Catholic parish. He faked credentials, stamped an official-looking seal on papers from the Diocese of Phoenix, and presented himself as Father Frederico. The diocese was desperate for a priest who spoke Spanish, so they took him without questions or a background check.

When Father Fred left after being discovered, the results were devastating. People who were married by the priestly impostor had to remarry. "By pretending to be a priest, Fred Brito played with the souls of people who trusted him," said Father Thomas Zurcher, vicar for priests in the Diocese of Phoenix. "In doing so he compounded their hurt and shriveled their spirit. He faked being nice when in fact he was a mean-spirited person who lived without regard for others."[19]

Authenticity is not possible without the bedrock belief of a larger purpose that identifies what and who we will be.

■ A "Larger Purpose" story . . .

We find the evidence stuffed in the back of her closet. Noticing the disappearance of several of our 13-year-old daughter's photos from the wall of fame in the hallway next to her room, we are dismayed to discover she has removed them. Her reason is simple; they embarrass her.

We try to explain. These are some of our most precious memories. She is unmoved by our soothing words and sentimental images. We are just Mom and Dad. To a teenager, honestly, what do we know?

I glance through the pictures of her scorn and glow with admiration and reminiscence. One is a Halloween picture where Christen is dressed as Casper the Friendly Ghost. Another is a beautiful shot of her at Radnor Lake in Nashville, Tennessee. Still another is a collection of the cousins surrounding their grandfather. Christen leans confidently into his arms, a white bow sitting atop her head. There is a serious one with her sitting and reading and then my favorite, an ear-to-ear grin showing proudly a chipped tooth as she models a head-full of pink sponge curlers. Oh, what a sight!

Somewhere along the way of teenage hormones and adolescent cool, she loses or misplaces the beauty of those photographic moments. Her teenage years take their toll and she experiences a self-image re-evaluation.

We all experience it. We do not like what we see in the mirror. We begin stuffing the pictures, disowning our past and disconnecting our future. It happens until someone, someday . . . convinces us to pull the pictures out of the dust and darkness of our closet and allow them to speak again. It happens until someone, someday . . . shows us not simply a picture of the future, but a picture of our larger purpose in that future.

Our new and eager teenager is lost in the sandstorm of her search for purpose and meaning. Her changing physical appearance plays havoc with her grasping attempt to identify what and who she will be within the tension of her disappearing childhood and beckoning womanhood. As a follower of Christ, I cannot miss the parallel of my Christian faith with this larger purpose story.

Christianity, at its core, is about a Heavenly Father who sends His son to do a once-and-for-all closet inspection. This Heavenly Closet Inspector stands at the door of your closet and knocks gently but persistently. He will not barge in to confront you. He will not point a finger condemning you. He will not embarrass you.

However, he will take pictures of a dusty and embarrassed past and redeem it. He will take pictures of a small, self-centered life and invite us into the studio of His grace and offer a portrait of a large, purpose-driven life. He will, with your surrender and willingness, touch-up every frailty and color in every empty spot as you paint an incredible larger purpose story of faith and forgiveness, lived in the brilliance of an authentic life.

■ A "Larger Purpose" travesty . . .

Any attempt to understand authentic relationships within the context of a larger purpose worldview must recognize what some have called the celebrification of culture. It is commonly defined as "the introduction of celebrity as a factor in some field or discipline." A supersized word, not unlike industrialization and bureaucratization, it identifies a broad and historical trend where celebrities are not simply trend-setters, but culture commentators and role models.

Joseph Epstein recognizes that "a received opinion about America in the early twenty-first century is that our culture values only two things: money and celebrity."[20] This influence of celebrity extends to taste, morality and public opinion.

Longtime writer for *Time* magazine, Richard Schickel identifies the pervasiveness of this impact: "possibly the most vital shaping (that is to say, distorting) force in our society."[21]

In the book, *Fame Junkies,*[22] Jake Halpern questions this obsession:

- Why do more people watch the ultimate competition for celebrity, *American Idol,* than watch the nightly news on the three major networks combined?
- Why do down-to-earth, educated people find stories about Paris Hilton's MORE CURRENT PERSON dating life irresistible?
- Why do teenage girls, when given the option of pressing a magic button to become either stronger, smarter, famous or more beautiful overwhelming choose fame?

The writer's use of the word "junkies" speaks to the real concern with this trend. Defined as "a person who gets an *unusual* amount of pleasure from or has an *unusual* amount of interest in something," a junkie, by their nature, is a person always in need of a larger purpose. Simply put, when a person's larger purpose is found *outside* of an *inside* personal satisfaction or peace, then authenticity will be an ongoing struggle.

Is it any wonder we struggle with authenticity?

Strong Point of View . . . Identify the price and power of choices

The third ingredient of authenticity Breen identifies is a strong point of view. Within authentic relationships, this parallels the need to identify the price and power of choices.

As a pastor for over four decades, my stories of people who have difficulty identifying and understanding the power of choices and the consequences of pain are legion. Novelist, poet, academic and Christian apologist C. S. Lewis' words speak to the issue of pain: "God whispers in our pleasures, speaks in our conscience, but shouts in our pain."[23] That said, many people soundproof their ears to God's whispers and live inauthentic lives because they never completely come to grips with an honest understanding about pain and consequences.

A life-principle I teach from the book of Acts is one I unearthed years ago and identify in many people. The principle is this: The truth about consequences is; the way of least resistance isn't without pain and the way of most resistance isn't without pleasure.

A study of Acts 21 shows the apostle Paul needing to decide about a trip to Jerusalem. Paul is warned not to go. With the last gasp of Jewish nationalism in the air, Paul will meet great opposition and possible death. Biblical scholars suspect Paul will encounter more violence than even Jesus since Paul is covering more territory and making Christianity more explicit and unmistakable. Their assumption is, if Paul lives, Judaism as it is would disappear.

Paul's friends urge him not to go because they care more about his personal safety than his cause, which he unfailingly serves. Ultimately, Paul chooses to go because he realizes there would be greater pain in not going, even though there is certain pain in going. The principle he chooses to live is simple, but not easy: the truth about consequences is the way of most resistance is not without pleasure.

Analysis of Acts 21 also shows wherever Paul and his party of travelers go, small groups of fellow believer's care for them. From island to island in the Aegean Sea, they find hostels of hospitality in a sea of foreigners. Even among great resistance, Paul finds God's grace and goodness, and among great pain, Paul finds God's provision and pleasure.

Reflecting on an earlier passage in the book of Acts when Christ gave a message to Paul through Ananias at his conversion experience in Damascus (Acts 9:15-16), Paul accepts suffering for Christ's sake as a part of his heritage. How could Paul take the path of most resistance and find pleasure in doing it? It is because his purpose defines his pleasure. Pain is both measured and accepted based on a willingness to define and accept consequences within each person's purpose.

While Paul does not have a death wish, Paul does recognize the difference between wanting to die and being willing to die. He realizes dying for the thing that most matters is not nearly as painful as living for things that do not matter. His life screams the truth about consequences: the way of least resistance isn't without pain and the way of most resistance isn't without pleasure.

This truth translates powerfully within our desire to understand authenticity and the belief that authenticity is grounded in the need to identify the price: of choices and the power of pain.

■ A "Strong Point of view" story . . .

I remember the day and the conversation as if it ended just moments ago. My mother calls to give me an update on the prognosis of her recent pain and doctor visits. Tests and more tests culminate in a call that changes the trajectory of her life and mine. I write the following in my journal: "I never knew my life could be so radically changed by the mention of one simple six-letter word: cancer."

While incredible progress in cancer research and treatment has significantly reduced the fear and ultimate outcome of that six-letter word, my mother knows it is a likely death sentence for her. An early smoker and coal miner's daughter from Hazard, Kentucky, where not smoking is the exception, the doctor's report is a moratorium on her future.

The next few months, while peppered with tattered moments of disbelief and despair, I can honestly and gratefully say these months are sealed with a strong point of view regarding her choices and her pain. Her choice to smoke is not as much a regret as her choice about when she quit. My mother struggles with quitting for years but is ultimately able to stop about four and a half years before she dies.

Her commitment to Christ is the turning point. Her transition from a grief-scarred, single parent, who marries for money to support her kids, to a Bible-reading, joy-seeking follower of Christ about five years before she dies. It is that strong point of view which translates her "regret" pain into "relief" pleasure. While I never heard my mother say as many cancer survivors say, "I thank God for my cancer," I did hear her say, "I thank God for my life." Her strong point of view for life as it was, not as she hoped for, culminated in her living every day for the rest of her life in fearless authenticity.

This point of view came from a lady who dealt with more pain, both self-imposed and circumstantially induced, than anyone I have known in her short fifty-six years on this earth. The journey with my Mom reaffirmed my belief that the way of least resistance is not without pain and the way of most resistance is not without pleasure.

■ A "Strong Point of View" travesty . . .

I am the new pastor of my first full-time church. Standing at the back door of the sanctuary after worship, I receive the welcome and admiration of the congregation as they pass through the door. Then I meet John. John Weigant, a man well into his 70s, pulls my outstretched hand toward him and whispers: "I want you to know, my wife's name was

Frances and I doubt if I will be able to stay at this church and constantly hear her name mentioned."

I am stunned, but quickly offer my condolences as my day of joy and exhilaration dissipates in the air like a punctured balloon. I remind him that our names are not spelled the same and that my name is a last name while his wife's was her first name, but his strong point of view is as closed as his wife's casket.

I later ask my staff and church members about John and with a roll of eyes and nodding of heads, they confirm his grief, now years in the making. I talk with John several times but quickly discover he lives in a small room with his view. His grief, rather than a balm of gratitude for years with his wife, is a prison of pain, built on a foundation of regret. From that imprisoned position, the only way to remember his wife is to grieve his loss at all cost to him personally. He did eventually leave the church because of my last name, Francis.

A strong point of view can serve either as a hinge of hope into a room of healing or a locked prison filled with defiant grief amid the choice of a gratifying life.

How about the story of Georgene Johnson? At the time of this writing, she lives in Cleveland, Ohio. She is 42 years old when she starts running and exercising to keep in shape. She says, "I'm not going to look like I am 42, or at least I am going to look like a good 42."

She does well in her running. She runs farther every day. She tries a little competition and enters a 10K race (about six miles). Nervous about her first race, she gets up early to arrive for the start of the race. To her surprise, many people are milling around, stretching, getting ready. All of a sudden, a voice on the microphone blares, "Move to the starting line." This is it. A gun sounds and they are off, like a huge wave, hundreds of runners, sweeping her into the moving masses.

After four miles it occurs to her that she ought to be reversing back to the finish line. She asks an official, "Why aren't the runners turning around?" He says, "Ma'am, you are running the Cleveland Marathon."

Remember, a marathon is slightly more than twenty-six miles. Her event, the 10K, it turns out, started a half-hour after the start of the marathon.

Most of us would have stopped, but to her credit, she keeps going and finishes the race. Her later reflection is profound: "This is not the race I trained for. This is not the race I entered. But for better or worse, this is the race that I am in."[24] That is a healthy point of view for whatever race in life we run.

A modern story of this premise about consequences, choices and pain is found in the life of great Argentine golfer, Robert De Vincenzo.[25] After winning a tournament, receiving the check and smiling for the cameras, he went to the clubhouse and prepared to leave. As he walked alone to his car, a young woman approached him. She congratulated him on his victory and then told him her child was seriously ill and near death. She did not know how to pay the doctor's bills and hospital expenses.

Touched by her story, De Vincenzo took out a pen and endorsed his winning check for payment to the woman. "Make some good days for the baby," he said as he pressed the check into her hand.

While having lunch in a country club the following week, a Professional Golf Association official came to his table. "Some of the boys in the parking lot last week tell me you met a young woman there after you won that tournament." De Vincenzo nodded.

"Well," said the official, "I have news for you. She's a phony. She has no sick baby. She's not even married. She fleeced you, my friend."

"You mean there is no baby who is dying?" questioned De Vincenzo.

"That's right," answered the official.

"That's the best news I've heard all week," De Vincenzo concluded with a smile.

What we see here is the incredible power of every person's point of view. Instead of seeing his financial loss and disappointment of being fleeced by a con artist, DeVincenzo chooses to see the gain of knowing there is no sick child.

From the weary apostle Paul to my cancer-ridden, single mom, to a grief-captured, widowed man, to a 40ish lady in an unplanned marathon and an accomplished, Hall of Fame golfer who wins in the end, we see the overwhelming power of a strong point of view.

Choices, consequences and pain are the ingredients for a perspective of life that either results in authenticity or artificiality. Which will you choose?

Integrity . . . Identify the ecstasy of alignment

Fourth, Bill Breen says authenticity involves integrity.[26] He notes when fast food giant, McDonald's, launched its "We love to see you smile" campaign, critics shook their heads in disgust, noting that filthy restrooms and crabby counter clerks turned the motto into a joke.

In order for a company or a person to be authentic, there must an alignment of values and methods. There must be integrity. Originating from the Latin "integer" meaning whole or complete, integrity thrives on the consistency of words and actions, declarations and outcomes.

The closer we align who we want to be with who we are, the more energy we have to establish and maintain healthy relationships.

Integrity is to relationships what pilot lights are to hot air balloons. Just as hot air balloons utilize a pilot light to assure rapid access to the heat needed to lift and control the vessel's motion and ultimate safety, relationships utilize integrity to insure consistent alignment of the values needed to clarify and guide the relationship's development and eventual maturity.

■ An "Integrity" story and travesty . . .

One is named Bubba. The other is named Bobby. One is on top of the world. The other is not. One smiles into the face of his wife and newly adopted son. The other looks away from the face of his wife and four children.

First, there is Bubba. Bubba Watson, the lefty, long-hitting American, who never took a golf lesson, is the 2012 Masters champ. For the uninitiated, winning the Masters golf tournament at Augusta National Golf Club in Augusta, Georgia is like winning the Super Bowl. To understand the power of this moment, you must understand the Augusta National Golf Club.

The club opened for play in 1933 and since 1934, it has played host to the annual Masters Tournament, one of the four major championships in professional golf and the only major played each year at the same course. Its exclusive membership policies have drawn criticism, particularly the refusal to admit black members until 1990. A former policy required all caddies to be black. Only since 2012 were women invited to join. Indeed, the Augusta National Golf Club put the "E" in exclusive.

As *Sports Illustrated* writer, Alan Shipnuck penned, "Augusta National may be a bastion of the 1%, but Watson is a down-home guy with a homemade golf swing whose dream car is the General Lee, the hot rod from *The Dukes of Hazzard*, which he recently bought at auction and has been tooling around in ever since."[27] After winning the tournament on the second hole of a sudden death playoff, he thanked the Georgia Bulldogs (his alma mater), Jesus Christ ("my Lord and savior") and the host club's African American locker room attendants, members of the 99% that make up Bubba's core constituency.

While unlikely, Bubba's win is no fluke. At 313.1 yards, he is the PGA Tour's longest hitter by almost six yards. He swings a driver with a macho pink head and shaft for cancer awareness, and for all four rounds at the Masters, his attire is all white, supporting children with disabilities.

Appropriate to the moment, Bubba won the Masters out of the trees. On the second playoff hole, he hooked his drive in a forest of pines off the fairway of the 10th hole. However, his motto has always been, "If I got a swing, I got a shot." He locates a gap in the trees and whipsaws what he calls a "40-yard hook" to within 15 feet of the hole, a small miracle.

As he pulls the final golf ball out of the hole, he falls into the arms of his caddie and then his mother, Molly. Noticeably absent is his wife, Angie, who is usually a towering presence in Bubba's entourage. A former WBNA player, she stands an inch taller than her 6' 3" husband. She stayed in Florida to care for their 6-week-old adopted son, Caleb. No wonder when asked if this is a dream come true, Bubba said, "I never got this far in my dreams."

Then there is Bobby. Bobby Petrino is the fired football coach at the University of Arkansas.[28] On April Fool's Day, 2012, he commits the ultimate fool's errand when he tries to get people to believe ridiculous things.

Petrino is involved in a single-vehicle accident on his Harley Davidson where he suffers broken ribs and other injuries, but attempts to cover up other facts released days later in a police report. He later confesses to having a passenger, 25-year-old Jessica Dorrell, a football employee with whom he is having an inappropriate relationship.

Petrino's initial account of the accident is that he was alone, 20 miles away from campus, after a day at the lake with his wife. He and Dorrell ask a driver, who approaches to see a bloodied Petrino struggling out of a ditch not to call 9-1-1. Although he goes out of his way to refer to his relationship with Jessica Dorrell in the past tense when he is put on paid leave, cellphone records show the pair stay in almost-daily contact after the motorcycle accident.

An investigation later shows Dorrell is hired by Petrino out of a pool of 158 candidates and given a $20,000 payment from personal funds. Arkansas' athletic director says the interview and hiring process for Dorrell was atypical to normal university practice. The young lady plays volleyball at Arkansas and is engaged to the university swimming and diving operations director, Josh Morgan, who reportedly left that job after news of the affair came to light.

Petrino has a history of controversial departures from previous places of employment. He bolted from the National Football League's Atlanta Falcons less than one year into a 10-year, $26 million contract at the University of Louisville and months later fled the NFL for Fayetteville, leaving notes in lockers of players and coaches to inform them of his decision to take the Arkansas job. His contract at Arkansas had an annual salary of $3.5 million, but because he was fired with cause, he did not receive a buyout or settlement. One of his final statements said it all: "As a result of my personal mistakes, we will not get to finish our goal of building a championship program."[29]

One is named Bubba. The other is named Bobby. One is on top of the world. The other is not. One smiles into the face of his wife and newly adopted son. The other looks away from the face of his wife and four children. What makes the difference between Bubba and Bobby? It is choices. It is relationships. It is integrity.

Think about it. One is a story of a dream not even imagined coming true. The other is a story of a cover-up not covered up. Mark it well. What you *say* is who you want to be and what you *do* is who you are!

So, is it possible to live a life of authenticity?

The apostle Paul offers an alternative to faking our way through life. He invites us to live blamelessly in every relationship (1 Thessalonians 2:9-12). Blameless is often misunderstood as a call to perfection. Actually, it is another way of saying . . . Live a life that is real so at the end of the day, you realize the ecstasy of aligning personal values and choices. Blameless is the opposite of faking it. When we pretend to be someone we are not, it is impossible to experience the elation of authenticity.

In Margery Williams' book, *The Velveteen Rabbit,* the author chronicles the story of a stuffed rabbit and his desire to become real through the love of his owner. There is a fascinating conversation between the Skin Horse and the Rabbit:

"What is Real?" asks the Rabbit one day, when they are lying side by side near the nursery fender, before Nana comes to tidy the room. "Does it mean having things that buzz inside you and a stick-out handle?"

"Real isn't how you are made" said the Skin Horse. "It's something that happens to you. When a child loves you for a long, long time, not just to play with, but really loves you, then you become real."

"Does it hurt?" asks the Rabbit. "Sometimes," answers the Skin Horse, for he is always truthful. "When you are real, you don't mind being hurt." "Does it happen all at once, like being wound up," he asks, "or bit by bit?"

"It doesn't happen all at once," said the Skin Horse. "You become. It takes a long time. That's why it doesn't often happen to people who break easily, or have sharp edges, or have to be carefully kept. Generally, by the time you are real, most of your hair has been loved off, and your eyes drop out and you get loose in the joints and very shabby. But these things don't matter at all, because once you are real you can't be ugly, except to people who don't understand."[30]

2

"Boundaries: Can I really tell you what I need?"

BOUNDARIES: STRENGTH TRAINING FOR DECISION-MAKING

"Boundaries are to protect life, not to limit pleasures."[31]

Edwin Louis Cole

"No is a complete sentence."[32]

Anne Lamott

Introduction

HIS NAME IS Charlie and I am not sure about him. He suddenly appears at our house and makes my mom smile again. Visits soon extend to overnights and before I know it, I have a step-dad. I barely knew my real dad, so how am I going to accept him as a step-dad? My Mom answers that question with "not very well."

She does not say it out loud, but it is clear. He is her husband and the "step" nature of his role in my life is limited to provision for our family and direction from my mom. I am not told to call him "dad." I am not to receive discipline and direction from him. Simply put, I am her blood and not his. That matters to a grief-stricken young mother from the coal mines of Hazard, Kentucky.

Predictably, I am rather neutral about him being around until one day, he invites me to go hunting with him. Let me be clear. I am absolutely sure I did not go hunting of my own volition. While my grandfather, Dadi, who lived many years with us was quite the outdoorsman, I did not share his admiration for guns and hunting. The choice was not mine, but I was prodded to give it a try.

I do not remember much about the handling of the gun or the discovery of rabbits and squirrels. I do remember being alone with Charlie when he asks if I need to go to the restroom. I say "yes" and he joins me as I remove my body from my clothes. I do not remember what he says, but I will never forget what he does. He touches me and explains how I can touch myself to feel certain sensations.

Ensuing internal trauma is an understatement. Questions. Guilt. Shame. However, I do not mention this to my mother, for fear she would use the .38 in her purse. Obviously, I never go hunting again.

This is my first memory of broken boundaries. Years later, while reading the book, *Boundaries,* by Henry Cloud and John Townsend, the whole experience resurfaces, like a bolt of lightning, exposed from my guarded mental pictures of childhood.

The reading of *Boundaries* influenced many of the insights in this chapter. I have given countless copies to clients during counseling, particularly to women, because in my experience, they tend to be more open to counsel, more relational and honest in expressing feelings about broken boundaries. Many copies have been placed in hands of women who undervalue themselves. Many are attractive and confident in the workplace, but lack fortitude when it comes to male relationships. Typically, a woman meets a man, then experiences a fairy tale feeling of romance, usually resulting in sexual intimacy before mature emotional intimacy has been formed. Often disappointment follows from a potential lack of respect. As a result, she must re-establish her crumbled boundaries.

Less dramatic, but as true, is the story Henry Cloud[33] tells of the parents of a 25-year-old man: They wanted to "fix" their son, Bill. When asked where he was, they answered, "Oh, he didn't want to come." "Why?" "Well, he doesn't think he has a problem." "Maybe he is right. Tell me about it."

They recited a history of problems starting at a young age. Bill, the son, is never quite up to snuff in their eyes and begins using drugs which results in an indifference with school and career options.

He is given everything . . . money for school, enough so he would not have to work. When he flunks out of one school, they send him to another. After a while, Henry stops them and says, "I think your son is right. He doesn't have a problem. You do. You pay, you fret, you worry, you plan, and you exert energy to keep him going. He doesn't have a problem because you have taken it from him. Would you like me to help you help him to have some problems?"

They took a deep breath and asked, "What do you mean?" He said, "I think the solution to this problem would be to clarify some boundaries so that his actions cause him problems and not you." Their confused expressions are proof they need further illustration.

"Look at it this way. It is as if he's your neighbor, who never waters his lawn. But, whenever you turn on your sprinkler system, the water falls on his lawn. Your grass is turning brown and dying, but Bill looks down at his green grass and thinks to himself, 'My yard is doing fine.' That is how your son's life is. He doesn't study, or plan or work, yet he has a nice place to live, plenty of money, and all the rights of a family member who is doing his part.

"If you would define the property lines a little better, if you would fix the sprinkler system so that the water would fall on your lawn, and if he didn't water his own lawn, he would have to live in dirt. He might not like that after a while. As it now stands, he is irresponsible and happy, and you are responsible and miserable. A little boundary clarification would do the trick."[34]

AUTHENTICITY BREEDS BOUNDARIES

A key result of honest authenticity is appropriate boundaries. However, before we talk about the ingredients for appropriate boundaries, it is important to reflect back on the **Stay in the Room** diagram identified in the previous chapter. Each of the corner experiences of fear, hurt, vengeance and blame represent opportunities either to build or break boundaries.

In my research on boundaries, I also read Charles L. Whitfield's book, *Boundaries and Relationships: Knowing, Protecting and Enjoying the Self*.[35] Dr. Whitfield is a bestselling author and psychotherapist who merges theories and dynamics from several disciplines into a strategy for understanding and improving relationships.

I found Dr. Whitfield's treatment of fear in relationships especially insightful. He also develops this in one of his other books, *Feelings and Wisdom to Know the Difference*. He bluntly states, "fear is an almost totally unnecessary feeling. In all practicality, it has almost no usefulness."[36]

He qualifies his comments by recognizing that fear can be useful in some emergency situations to sound the alarm of awareness, but "in most situations, and certainly from a higher and spiritual perspective, it is not useful. We either create fear (most of it), it is inflicted upon us (some of it), or both (a lot of it)."[37] Dr. Whitfield's advice is not to deny fear when it inevitably comes, but rather "to feel the fear, recognize it, identify it and decide whether it has any usefulness at all for us at that moment."[38]

The more I listen to those with boundary issues, the more I am convinced that all of the identified feelings in the **Stay in the Room** diagram should be considered in a similar fashion. Fear, hurt, vengeance and blame should all be identified as feelings that may be useful to bring awareness of a possible boundary breach, but they are not useful if we seek to attain a "higher (and) spiritual perspective" within our relationships. This quote, "higher (and) spiritual perspective," is a significant qualifier to understanding how we can get out of the corner of relationships burdened by fear, hurt, vengeance and blame and get to the table of reconciliation in all our relationships.

As I write these words, many quality leaders are dealing with boundary breaches in their working environment. As CEO's, ministers, teachers and countless others know, a breach threatens essential purposes needed for success. There are always going to be those in search of power; those who need it for edification and/or ego. Speaking from many experiences in church environments, needy parasites damage our message and the Body of Christ. The church seems a safe haven to exert power as a volunteer who cannot be fired. As a leader, confrontation in church threatens the very peace and love every parishioner seeks. So it is with fear and trembling that many ministers and other leaders in vulnerable positions walk the fine line of setting and enforcing healthy boundaries.

By nature, I am a confronter. The one thing about coming from a dysfunctional family life is everything was on the table. Feelings were not spared, and words were certainly not minced. There can be hurt in that, but there is also an honesty that is raw. No one is feeling your emotional pulse to see if you are happy, secure, or even safe. It is no surprise that confrontation for me is like breathing and painful as it may be, breathing is better than the alternative.

Following an adequate time for processing a situation, a good leader must confront. Not dealing with an issue is to delay the inevitable. People take their places in the corners of the room, licking the wounds of their hurt feelings and wallowing in the fear, vengeance, and blame of their respective versions of the issue at hand.

Like all relationships, we have two choices. We can hold on to feelings of hurt and vengeance and look for opportunities to return sniper shots or use feelings to lead to a spiritual perspective.

Using the **Stay in the Room** analogy (as seen in the diagram), we can invite people to the table of reconciliation. They will have the option either to reject or to come and sit quietly, waiting for the reconciliation talk. A spiritual perspective demands we use our feelings of hurt and vengeance like pumping weights in a gym; to build strength for decision-making that allows us to have strong boundaries in all our relationships.

My mind drifts to a popular song from my teenage years. I was sweating acne and sporting bellbottom pants when I first heard the Rolling Stones' sing, "You Can't Always Get What You Want." Named the top 100 greatest song of all time by the *Rolling Stone* magazine in 2004, it was written by the classic rockers, Mick Jagger and Keith Richards.[39]

The three topics discussed in the song address the hot button of the 1960s and 1970s: love, politics and drugs. It is the movement in the song that I find interesting. There is a unique mixture of optimism, disappointment, and finally, there is an acquiescent practicality that saves the day:

You can't always get what you want
You can't always get what you want
You can't always get what you want
But if you try sometimes well you just might find
You get what you need

Our relationships always arrive with some sense of optimism. Who is this person? What are they like? What do we want from this relationship or on a deeper level, what do we need from this relationship? At some point along the way in every relationship, conflict and likely some sense of disappointment enters into the dynamic of determining what we want and what we need with this relationship. Too often, as identified in the previous graphic, we resort to fear, hurt, vengeance and blame. But, hopefully, we realize no matter how real these feelings are, they are just feelings that we can either use for a spiritual perspective (purpose) or we can wallow in the need to be right and lose our friends and foes, to petty differences. I propose we choose **Stay in the Room** relationships. While we "can't always get what we want," we can, with a higher spiritual perspective, "get what we need."

The goal of this chapter is to define what a healthy boundary is and then to determine how to develop boundaries that not only allow us to showcase **Stay in the Room** relationships, but also answer the question, "Can I really tell you what I need?" What we will discover is just as establishing authenticity was soul training for transparency, building boundaries is based on strength training for decision-making.

BAGGAGE CLAIM

My wife, Neva, and I enter the room rolling one piece of luggage each. Smiles and giggles follow our entrance to the front of the room. As we have done many times, we are teachers for a marriage enrichment retreat and are preparing to share our experience with baggage and boundaries. While this suitcase session is more about baggage, boundaries are the natural consequence of identifying the baggage each person carries into the intimacy of a marriage relationship.

Neva pulls out a Cinderella book and describes how this story details her view of courtship and marriage. I pull out a picture of my blended family and explain that my mother was widowed with three young children before she married three times and had three more children.

Neva pulls out a college diploma and explains she never remembers a time in her life when she did not believe she would go to college because that is what her brothers and sisters did. I pull out a high school diploma and share that I was the only one of two from the six children in my family who graduated from high school and the only one who went on to college and graduate school.

Neva pulls out a picture from one of her sister's weddings and shares that she always knew she would have a big church wedding. She further explains that her white dress signifies she would be a virgin when she got married. I pull out a condom because my sex education consisted of my mother telling me to go out and have my way with any woman that would allow it, but marry the one who would not. Also, not only had I never seen a church wedding, I did not have a clue about long-term relationships, having never witnessed one.

You get the picture. Miss Polly Pure Heart meets Wild and Crazy Dan. That would be true except my life radically changed about four years before I met Neva and most of my extreme baggage had been emptied, then refilled with something significantly different. However, I would not be truthful if I said we did not deal with baggage issues, in particular, the role of our family to her family and the way we deal with anger and disagreement.

With regards to anger, Neva grew up in a home of carpet sweepers and I survived a home of table screamers! Neva grew up with very little anger outwardly expressed. If disagreement arose, then all parties did their best to stuff their frustrations under the carpet, knowing that it was unlikely to ever be discussed. I grew up with a mother who had no filters for her anger or language. If she thought it, she said it and if she felt it, well, you were likely to feel something as well. Anger was thrown on the table and profanely screamed out. Then life slowly went back to normal.

Just how important is baggage for our study of boundaries? It is absolutely crucial. All my research, both experientially and educationally, confirm that we learn most about personal boundaries from our family of origin. Family of origin refers to the significant caretakers and siblings a person grows up with or the first social group to which a person belongs, often a person's biological or adoptive family. More times than not, we are either a product of or a reaction to what we experience in our family of origin.

But then something happens. We grow up and leave our families and begin to negotiate how we will develop. Tragically, many people never really leave home, even though their address changes. They are a conglomerate of the collective influences experienced in their family of origin. Their boundaries are disjointed and incoherent.

No one grows up in a family of origin that has perfect boundaries, but for those who marry well or those who have the strength to surround themselves with friends who challenge their old family of origin boundaries, something happens.

If the married couple is tied to a church tradition for their wedding, then they will likely identify the scriptural admonition to leave, cleave and weave. Having done more than a few weddings and the counseling inherent in most of them, I can tell you making the move from family of origin to what I call the family of opportunity is a cavernous leap. Family of opportunity is the result of the merging of the families of origin and inherent in this merging is the identification and assessment of boundaries.

While this family of opportunity is easier to identify in marriage settings, it is just as real for other groupings of people who do life together. Identify any person or group who live within your sphere of influence (in other words, they influence you and you influence them), and this person or persons will have a place in your family of opportunity. One of the major tasks of incorporating these new influencers will be identifying baggage and constructing new boundaries.

Anne Linden, author of the book, *Boundaries in Human Relationships: How to Be Separate and Connected,* speaks to the importance of this journey when she says, "The most important distinction anyone can ever make in their life is between who they are as an individual and their connection with others."[40] As we transition from our family of origin to our family of opportunity, the key and ongoing question will be, "Can I really tell you what I need?" If this question does not receive an affirmative answer, then the strength needed for decision-making, which builds strong boundaries, will not be possible.

DEFINING BOUNDARIES

So, what is a relational boundary? I have fashioned one from several different sources:

"Personal boundaries are the physical, emotional and mental parameters we create to protect ourselves from being manipulated, exploited, or violated by others. They allow us to separate who we are, and what we think and feel, from the thoughts and feelings of others. Their presence helps us express ourselves as the unique individual we are, while we acknowledge the same in others."

While Cloud and Townsend do not offer a simple definition of boundary, they do describe how a boundary works:

- Boundaries define us. They define what is me and what is not me.[41]
- Boundaries are not walls.[42]
- The most basic boundary-setting word is no.[43]

They also offer a comprehensive list of boundaries: skin, words, truth, geographical distance, time, emotional distance, other people, consequences, feelings, attitudes and beliefs, behaviors, choices, values, limits, talents, thoughts, desires, and love. From here, they distinguish the overlying premise for their book: we must take responsibility for all the boundaries in our lives.

The most powerful section of the book for our purposes, however, is found in chapter five where the writers describe the Ten Laws of Boundaries. While the scope of that section exceeds the purposes of this book, law number ten, The Law of Exposure, could not be more germane to our journey.

"The Law of Exposure says that your boundaries need to be made visible to others and communicated to them in relationship."[44] Because of the feelings of fear, hurt, vengeance and blame discussed earlier, we can have secret and often unacknowledged boundaries. We withdraw, resent and experience the pain of someone's irresponsibility instead of being honest about how irresponsibility impacts us.

It should surprise no one that unexpressed boundaries result in weakened relationships and various conflicts. If we are unable to expose our need for boundaries in an honest and direct way, our feelings of fear, blame, vengeance and hurt will be communicated indirectly (passive-aggressive behavior) or through some level of manipulation.

The whole premise of **Stay in the Room** relationships is to find a way and a time to make sure people see us clearly and honestly. Boundaries are the amplifiers for our feelings to be seen and heard and if the volume of our needs and desires are muted through our discomfort over sharing them, then we begin to live a dual life where we hide parts of ourselves in the darkness.

Cloud and Townsend say, "When our boundaries are in the light, that is, are communicated openly, our personalities begin to integrate for the first time. They become 'visible' in Paul's words and then they become light. They are transformed and changed. Healing always takes place in the light."[45]

This can be an empowering insight for the person who struggles with having honest relational boundaries. Dishonest relational boundaries produce relational chameleons, who change their message and tone depending on who they are with and in what situation they find themselves. Just as chameleons can change colors by adjusting a layer of special cells nestled within their skin, boundary-weak people change the colors of their boundaries and communication to thwart the fear of losing people through rejection or abandonment.

Left unattended, this color-coding for fear of losing relationships will result in a person who hides their true feelings and ultimately loses the battle to be authentic. Remember, authenticity, the plea for identity that asks the transparent, honesty question, "Can I really tell you who I am?" must be followed by the boundary-building question, "Can I really tell you what I need?" or our relational decision-making will be rendered weak and destructive. Healthy, whole relationships must have strong, defined boundaries. So, how do we develop these boundaries?

DEVELOPING BOUNDARIES: ACCOUNTABILITY

It is impossible to develop boundaries without a clear and concise understanding of accountability, and yet, the word accountability can carry negative connotations. Accountability brings a heightened sense of expectations and expectations increase anxiety. So, what does accountability really mean and how can we use it to assist in the arduous task of developing healthy boundaries?

Three Latin words shape the original meaning of accountability:

- *accomptare* means "to account"
- *computare* means "to calculate"
- *putare* means "to reckon."

The origin of the word accountable in the English language occurs sometime between the early part of the 14th century and the late 16th century. In any event, that early English usage is not far from a current dictionary definition of accountable, an adjective meaning: "subject to the obligation to report, explain or justify something; answerable." The noun accountability, first appearing in the late 18th century, is defined by the Merriam Webster Dictionary as follows: "the quality or state of being accountable; especially an obligation or willingness to accept responsibility or to account for one's actions."

My use of the word accountable is based on my understanding that real-life accountability is not optional for any caring, connected, growing relationship built on authenticity and boundaries. If I am in a relationship where there is mutual and ongoing value, there will be an expectation of accountability.

If our most basic need beyond food and water is for relationships, then our need to belong to others and be in relationships is simply another way of saying, "I need to be counted." Even animals can demonstrate a need to belong and be counted. What is it about human beings and our need to be needed?

Think about it. That's right, think, because there is no other creature on planet earth that has our ability to think. So, if our need to be recognized is met, what comes next? Our thinking allows and I would even say, demands that we move from the need to be counted to understanding our ability to count.

We are not dogs, wagging our tails in sync with the affirmation of our masters, basking in the afterglow of just belonging. We are humans who need to belong, but also have the ability to count *how* we belong and *how* we become the best version of ourselves.

So, the starting point in establishing healthy boundaries is to be relationally aligned with the power of accountability. Accountability is the recognition that while we need to be counted and belong to others in authentic relationships, we also have the ability to count and find ways to live in boundary-building relationships.[46]

Many years ago, I heard the late Stephen Covey say in one of his seminars that "accountability breeds response-ability." This is another way of saying that we have "the ability to count" how our relationships can be strengthened through transparent authenticity and strong boundaries. Another way to identify and clarify this "ability to count" step is to recognize the power of awareness.

DEVELOPING BOUNDARIES: AWARENESS

The longer I live, the more I realize the astonishing power of awareness. Aristotle said as much when he declared that the "ultimate value of life depends upon awareness and the power of contemplation rather than upon mere survival."[47]

The word, awareness, however, is bland and falls on deaf ears without descriptive adjectives that add specificity and interpretation. I have landed on three such qualifiers that will assist in our understanding of how to develop boundaries through awareness.

Self-awareness

If self-awareness could speak it would say, "I am responsible for my thoughts and actions. It is not enough to know my thoughts and actions. I must be responsible for them."

We must be "self" aware and while this sounds easy, it is not. As previously referenced, the baggage of relationships weighs heavy in a person's battle to know and be themselves. Self-awareness is crucial as the starting point for relational accountability, but it is complicated and humbling. Simply put, an inability to identify our true feelings leaves us at the mercy of those feelings.[48]

Daniel Goldman, in his book, *Emotional Intelligence*, offers a pure and powerful example. When a child whose anger has led him to hit a playmate, we can stop the act of hitting, but we cannot suffocate the anger that caused it. Often the anger simmers and continues. Self-awareness has a powerful impact on feelings of anger: "because the simple understanding of anger brings a greater degree of freedom, not just the option to act on it, but the added option to let it go."[49]

Steward-awareness

If steward-awareness could speak it would say, "I am responsible for my knowledge and growth. It is not enough to know my thoughts and actions. As a good steward and manager of my mind, body and spirit, I must be responsible to grow in knowledge and in truth."

Steward-awareness declares war on the shrug of the shoulders approach to life that says, "that's just the way I am." Those who possess steward-awareness accept the fact that they alone are the overseers and arbiters of their lives. Steward-awareness is what drives the ongoing search for input and improvement in knowing and being accountable in all our relationships.

Honestly, the fact that you are reading this book shows you are making an attempt at being a good steward.

Spin-awareness

If spin-awareness could speak it would say "I am responsible for my assumptions and perceptions which means I will shine the 'distortion' light regularly and carefully onto my thoughts and actions, knowledge and growth."

The need for spin-awareness is a recent phenomenon, at least in my thinking. In the age of the Internet, Twitter and Facebook, many are encouraged to develop a personality and a brand for their "tribe." Often called "digital tribe," it is a term used to identify an unofficial community of people who share a common interest and are affiliated with each other through social media.

While this is an amazingly powerful tool for individuals to express themselves and receive input, the impersonal nature of these relationships can either over or undervalue a person. We must develop a spin-awareness that monitors and clarifies the assumptions and perceptions we know about ourselves.

So, how are you doing with self-awareness, steward-awareness and spin-awareness? My personal experience with assessing my relational boundaries in light of these levels of personal awareness, is that they give definition and distinction to where I need to grow and change.

BAGGAGE SCALES

Cloud and Townsend make a powerful distinction about the whole issue of baggage that is crucial for any boundary-balanced relationship. Drawing on an analysis of Greek words from the book of Galatians in the New Testament, they offer a practical word for understanding accountability and awareness. Their premise is important and worth remembering: We are responsible *to* others and *for* ourselves.

This idea is based on their understanding of Galatians 6:2: "Carry each other's burdens and in this way, you will fulfill the law of Christ." Clearly we have a responsibility to one another.

The important feature occurs later in verse five when it says, "each one should carry his own load." This seems to contradict what was previously stated in verse two until analysis of the Greek words for burden and load are explained.

The Greek word for burden means "excess burdens," or "burdens so heavy they weigh us down." These burdens are like boulders and they crush us. Without help from others, we will break!

In contrast, the Greek word for load means "cargo," or "the burden of daily toil." These loads are like knapsacks and they describe the everyday things we all need to do.[50]

The writers conclude two clarifying choices that are crucial for understanding and developing strong relational boundaries. The first choice is when people act as if their boulders are daily loads and refuse help, living with perpetual pain. The second choice is when people act as if their daily loads are boulders and believe they shouldn't have to carry them, becoming irresponsible.

Ask yourself how many people you know right now who could have their relationships significantly improved and even healed if the truth of the boulders and knapsacks could be understood in their lives?

CONCLUSION

Fred Craddock, who passed in March of 2015, was recognized as one of the twelve most effective preachers in the English-speaking world in a 1996 survey of seminary professors and editors. An ordained minister in the Christian church from rural Tennessee, most of his professional life was as Professor of Preaching and New Testament in the Candler School of Theology at Emory University in Atlanta, Georgia. The following story is classic Craddock and, in this case, I would encourage you to identify the broken relational branches of accountability and awareness.

Dr. Craddock was asked to go some distance to a meeting. A fellow was going to the same meeting, lived near, and asked, "You want a ride?" "Yeah, save me the gasoline, the wear and tear." "I will stop by and get you."

When he came by, in the back seat were his wife and daughter. The daughter had just graduated from college, a very attractive young woman. She said, "Sit up there and y'all can talk. We're not going to the meeting; we're just going shopping."

They started out on the 200-mile trip and had gotten about 25 miles when the man's wife, sitting right behind her husband said, "You're going too slow," so he sped up. Then she said, "You're going to kill us all." He slowed down. She said, "We'll never get there. Are you going to pass here?" So he didn't pass. She said, "Why are you waiting in line?" He started to pass around when she said, "Don't you see the yellow line? We're in the wrong lane."

Pick, pick, pick, pick, pick, pick. Pretty soon the daughter joined in and this man was sitting there in silence. Fred was embarrassed. What do you do? You don't want to be there. You'd rather be walking. So what do you do? He just sat there stewing. He said to himself: "If this fellow was a man, if he really were a man, he'd pull this car over and leave a couple. Then he and Fred could go to their meeting."

The further they traveled, the more he began to say to himself, "Now, if this fellow were a man..." When they got there, the wife and daughter went shopping. Fred and the man had a few minutes and the man asked, "You want some coffee?"

They went into a little place and sat there staring at the coffee. What do you say? How do you start a conversation?

Fred knew, the man knew and he knew that Fred knew. Honestly, what do you do? Fred just sat there staring at his coffee as though it was real interesting coffee.

Finally, the man said, "Fred, you teach in a seminary?" Fred said, "Yeah."

"I mean you are into religion and all that?"

"Yeah."

"I mean you know the Bible and Christianity."

"Yeah, what are you talking about?"

He said, "Well, I just wondered, in your study and in your opinion, what hope do you think there is for a man who has everything in life at the age of 50, *everything in life he wants, except the one thing he wants the most?*"[51]

Boundaries either protect us or pound us . . . and the decision, while never easy, is ultimately and personally ours. Whether it is about a little boy in the woods with an abusive step-dad or a husband humiliated by his wife and child, everyone needs boundaries.

3

Compatibility: "How can we get along if we are so different?"

COMPATIBILITY: RELATIONAL TRAINING FOR VULNERABILITY

"He and I were about as compatible as
a rat and a boa constrictor."[52]

Stevie Nicks

COMPATIBILITY BY ITS nature is a core ingredient for relational health because it neither feeds on or runs from conflict. Compatibility is the door into the room of every relationship that desires **Stay in the Room** perseverance as both a goal and a grace to loving vulnerability.

Why are we so dreadful at assessing and overcoming the conflict that can result in a reasonable opportunity for compatibility? A story might help.

"Let's go parasailing" sounds like a reasonable request from a reasonable man, (me), to a reasonable woman, my wife, Neva. There we are, two lovebirds resting on a Bahamian beach basking in our return to the sight of our honeymoon fifteen years earlier when I stir the pot of risk and adventure.

Before I go any further, allow me to explain, "parasailing." The word "para" comes from the Greek word meaning "beside" which means a person is a little "beside" himself to do this particular activity. "Para" may also mean "alteration" or "modification" when connected to another word. So, parasailing is a kind of sailing that has been altered or modified.

The honest truth is that parasailing is when people reluctantly allow themselves to be attached to a parachute pulled by a ski boat floating more than 200 feet in the air. And yes, someone actually pays for the joy of this frighteningly, joyful experience.

So, why would my bride and I choose to do this? For me, it is the fulfillment of a dream. On our honeymoon I wanted to parasail, but after hearing a young bride's plea not to be an early widow, I delayed my dream. For Neva, it is a kind of double-dare, pretty-please, in-the-heat-of-the-moment response to a begging husband. I think I say something romantic like, "Just think, if we go down, we will go down flying together!" No wonder she could not resist.

As the leaders of the expedition gather the thrill-seekers, I notice there are seven in our group. I am silently comforted knowing that seven is the biblical number for perfection or completion. As the leader stands looking at the hesitant hope plastered on our faces, he chooses Neva to be first. Good thing. For her it is better now than later. Matter of fact, the look on her face tells me it may need to be now or not at all. Before she can say, "Should I really do this," she begins her journey to the land of clouds and sunshine.

I watch as she quickly becomes airborne. Positioned in a cautious crouch, hands gripping the balloon-held guide-wires, she rides the wind until the rope is fully extended. Then it happens. She lets go.

Realizing she is secure in the harness, her death-grip loosens, and she begins to experience the magical ecstasy of floating in air. Arms waving freely, she begins to swing joyously in the wind tunnel of the air.

Once a picture of caution and concern, she is now a canvas of freedom and trust. Once a snapshot of uncertainty and fear, she is now a full-length movie of serendipitous joy. She makes the journey from the unknown to the known. Her words of reflection would be an offering to the obvious: "I wish I had let go sooner!"

What does she learn? She learns that holding on to the known, especially when it is based on fear and intimidation, limits our opportunity to experience the exhilaration of freedom and fun. Many of us are doing exactly that with our relationships, past and present.

Relationships typically follow the pattern of exploration we discover in this story.

- A *risk* is offered and a step is taken toward an unknown ("Let's go parasailing!").
- As the unknown is investigated, a decision is made to move forward producing a strong sense of *vulnerability* ("I am not sure I want to go through with this decision.").
- The length and depth of the vulnerability determines the level of *compatibility* possible for each relationship (Security in the parachute harness brings freedom and fun).

I define *vulnerability* as "the ability to be 'open' in relationships." I define *compatibility* as "the ability to 'complete' our relationships." I do not, however, mean, "complete" in the way we hear it portrayed in romantic ballads or movies, "you complete me!" I use it in the sense of completing the purpose that relationship has in a person's life. For instance, an incredibly difficult relationship at work may be "completed," not by leaving the job or seeing the person in the conflict being fired, but when a level of compatibility is achieved which satisfies work responsibilities without compromising the authenticity and boundaries of both parties.

Where do you struggle most in establishing and maintaining relationships? Do you struggle with the initial risk step and if so, why? Does this revolve around the issue of authenticity? Is vulnerability an overwhelming concern because your relational risk threatens your long-standing, healthy boundaries? Does having compatibility as a goal in all your relationships produce encouraging confidence or impossible dread?

Nice or New

As mentioned previously, most of my life has been providing leadership in the local church. Just as this chapter on compatibility is right in the middle of the book, the issue of compatibility is right in the middle of most difficulties that arise in the local church. I honestly don't think it is significantly different in the secular world. Matter of fact, compatibility is a dual threat in the church: it is a threat to those inside the church as well as those outside the church who are likely to make their decision about church based on the compatibility of those in the church.

My reason for writing this book is my experience with relational dysfunction and breakdown. My honest belief is this: there is no pain quite like relational breakdown and it comes in spades in the local church for two reasons:

1. The first reason relates to the heartbeat of the church. Birthed in love, the church lives to love and if those in the church cannot live in redemptive, loving relationships, then the church is not the church.

2. The second reason relates to the radical nature of being a follower of Christ. Many in the church confuse being a follower of Christ as being a little nicer than before they began a journey to follow Christ. Honestly, it breaks my heart to say this, but after decades in the local church, many people following Christ hope to be "nice," but "new" is not a serious option for them, especially in how they do relationships.

I will allow the words of C. S. Lewis to speak for me on Christ's desire NOT for nice, but new people.

"'Niceness'—wholesome, integrated personality—is an excellent thing. We must try by every medical, educational, economic, and political means in our power, to produce a world where as many people as possible grow up *nice*; just as we must try to produce a world where all have plenty to eat. But we must not suppose that even if we succeeded in making everyone *nice* we should have saved their souls. A world of *nice* people, content in their own niceness, looking no further, turned away from God, would be just as desperately in need of salvation as a miserable world-and might even be more difficult to save.

"For mere improvement is not redemption, though redemption always improves people even here and now and will, in the end, improve them to a degree we cannot yet imagine. God became man to turn creatures into sons: not simply to produce better men of the old kind but to produce a *new* kind of man."[53]

New Or Nothing

I have been teaching Matthew 18:15 for so long, it is difficult to know when Jesus' radical words on relationships became the desire of my heart and the practice of my life. The only freeze frame moment I can remember is hearing Bill Hybels, pastor of Willow Creek Community Church, share his heart a number of years ago.

I honestly suspect my understanding of Jesus' words in Matthew 18:15 came as a life-preserver to a drowning young pastor. Looking back on the reasons for my near drowning were simple and sad: leadership decisions bring disagreement, disagreement brings relational pain and relational pain in the church is difficult because we are supposed to be nice to one another.

This chapter on compatibility will revolve around the words of Jesus in Matthew 18:15 when he says, "And if there is a conflict/you/go/to the other person/in private and discuss/the problem/for the purpose of reconciliation."

I have placed a diagonal slash between sections of the verse to mark the seven words or phrases that will lead us through a process for "redemptive reconciliation."

I. THE MENTAL STEP—"IF THERE IS A CONFLICT"

The mental step is more difficult than it seems. The simple two letter word, "if," is fraught with misinterpretation. The primary confusion surrounds "who" more than "if." The "if" is often interpreted from the perspective of blame. The one-sided conversation usually goes this way: "Well, I don't have a conflict with that person" which is code for "well, they are the ones with a conflict not me, and besides that, I have been nice to them."

Acknowledgement of a problem, concern or issue is the essential starting point for any and all solutions of conflict. Thomas a Kempis, 15th century Augustinian priest and the likely author of the Christian classic, *The Imitation of Christ,* said, "The acknowledgment of our weakness is the first step in repairing our loss."[54] Later, American writer and journalist, Ambrose Bierce, would add, "Acknowledgement of one another's faults is the highest duty imposed by our love of truth."[55]

I have seen situations where no clear weakness or fault is identifiable, but there is still a conflict that left untended will fester and create distance between friends who simply happen to be on opposite sides of a situation.

Besides the "who" misinterpretation of the conflict issue, there is also the possible "conflict" misinterpretation. How we grow up handling conflict and anger will go a long way in dictating how we define conflict. Sometimes the fear of *any* conflict or the view that a lack of conflict is a sign of maturity will weaken the resolve of the injured party and they will hide it away without acknowledgement. While this appears to be harmless, stuffed conflict and anger will eventually resurface.

II. THE INITIATIVE STEP—"YOU"

This second step is one of ownership. It is more than acknowledging a problem might exist. In this step, one or both parties own a part of the conflict and acknowledge something needs to be done to resume clarity and consensus within the relationship.

Here I see a subtle but hopeful underlying shift from the "who" question, to the "whoever" possibility. Whoever implies that both parties will share either in the blame or the realization that *a* conflict exists. Instead of wallowing in the indecision of fault and blame, we move to the step of ownership and reconciliation.

Resistance to ownership of our responsibility is birthed by the rampant individualism of our age. Noted German-born psychiatrist and psychotherapist, Fritz Perls, wrote a 56-word "Gestalt Prayer" which highlighted the therapy he and his wife developed and it highlights fervent individualism:

"I do my thing and you do your thing.

I am not in this world to live up to your expectations,

And you are not in this world to live up to mine.

You are you, and I am I,

and if by chance we find each other, it's beautiful.

If not, it can't be helped."[56]

Megastar singer and songwriter, Beyonce, offers an updated version of this with a chorus from her song, "Me, Myself and I."

"Me, myself and I

That's all I got in the end

That's what I found out

And it ain't no need to cry

I took a vow that from now on

I'm gonna be my own best friend."[57]

The prayer and the song clearly speak to living in response to our own needs. They rub against the power and solidarity of deep and abiding interpersonal relationships vital to the kind of community sought within the local church, business community, or personal family and friends.

Walter Tubbs, a professor of Psychology and Philosophy at Johnston College in California responded to Fritz Perls declaration with one of his own:

Beyond Perls

If I just do my thing and you do yours,

We stand in danger of losing each other

And ourselves.

I am not in this world to live up to your expectations;

But I am in this world to confirm you

As a unique human being,

And to be confirmed by you.

We are fully ourselves only in relation to each other;
The I detached from a Thou
Disintegrates.

I do not find you by chance;
I find you by an active life
Of reaching out.

Rather than passively letting things happen to me,
I can act intentionally to make them happen.

I must begin with myself, true;
But I must not end with myself:
The truth begins with two.[58]

This writer offers a confident message of emotional and relational connectedness.

A resistance to relational ownership is not only fueled by individualism but has led to what may be the newest relational disease of our age, self-justification. That is the premise of the book, *Mistakes Were Made (But Not by Me)*, by Carol Tavris and Elliot Aronson. The writers say, "Most people, when directly confronted by evidence that they are wrong, do not change their point of view or course of action but justify it even more tenaciously. Even irrefutable evidence is rarely enough to pierce the mental armor."[59]

Swimming against the tide of individualism and self-justification makes it difficult to lift the need for ownership in relational conflict. But it must be done. The Initiative Step ("You") must be done if we are to live honestly and deeply, but I offer two words of caution:

1. If every conflict ends with a "go," we would be going more often than not. While we speak to this more in the chapter on discernment, sometimes even after we determine our part in the conflict, it may not be something that rises to the level of relational integrity.

In other words, some do conflict like they breathe. They are serial conflict offenders (SCO) with every relational breach, and this is a horrible waste of time and energy. When a SCO uses their natural inclination to conflict with such regularity and contempt that people are being bullied and bloodied, then something has to be done.

2. For people of faith, prayer is an indispensable resource for discernment regarding relationships. My former seminary professor, George Buttrick, wrote prolifically on the subject of prayer: *Prayer* and *The Power of Prayer Today*. Hear the following comments as preparation for taking the Initiative step.

"Prayer is not a vain attempt to change God's will; it is a filial (brotherly) desire to learn God's will and to share it. Prayer is not a substitute for work: it is the secret spring and indispensable ally of all true work."

"Intercession is more than specific: it is pondered: it requires us to bear on our heart the burden of those for whom we pray."

"Prayer is not a substitute for work, thinking, watching, suffering, or giving; prayer is a support for all other efforts."[60]

III. THE BEHAVIOR STEP—"GO"

Few make it to step three. Brave, bold and even obnoxious people still tremble with the thought of going to someone to talk about conflict. Notice my qualifier. Many of the before-mentioned folks scream and lash out and berate others over points of differences, but few of them actually go to someone to talk about conflict. My view is that "to talk" means they have processed their anger and understanding of the situation long enough to have a coherent and hopeful view of the disagreement.

Libraries could be filled with books on the nuances of confrontation, but ultimately, most of us do not confront because of some level of fear. We fear being misunderstood (some believe confrontation is the same as anger) and we fear that going will not make a difference. At the core of our fear is the belief that it is better to let sleeping dogs lie. I contend, however, it is an illusion to believe that sleeping dogs remain sleeping forever. Matter of fact, sleeping dogs do wake up and my preference would be to awaken the dog when I am ready to confront the dog, rather than wonder, wait and depend on the sleeping habits of the dog.

The decision to go is a decision to act and hopefully, it is based on the result of going through steps 1 and 2, which conclude, not to go is worse than to go. That is the contention of the book, *The Power of Decision*, where the author, Raymond Charles Barker, says, "Indecision is actually the individual's decision to fail."[61]

IV. THE PERSONAL STEP—"TO THE OTHER PERSON"

Up until this point, everything in the reconciliation process is an idea, an understanding or a concept. Now, everything gets personal. I like how John Eldredge says, "The life we have is so far from the life we truly want, (and) it doesn't take us long to find someone to blame."[62] So, we must personally approach the other person.

The litmus test of conflict resolution is not *if* but *how* we deal with other people. The "how" of conflict resolution is two-fold;

1. First, do we know enough about the person and the situation to approach the other person? Honestly, the first 3 steps should have answered this question.

2. Second, have we talked with other people about this issue? My experience tells me the chances of reconciliation are greatly diminished if other people are involved, unless, of course, they were a part of the original conflict.

Scripturally and personally, I believe the intention of this step is to limit the first discussion to No Third Parties. That conclusion is based on decades of seeing a reconciliation process interrupted and short-circuited because of the need to talk with other people before talking with the person originally and directly connected to the conflict.

When we find the need to bring in third parties, it is usually NOT in the name of objectivity ("I want to check the facts"), or spirituality ("I want to check my spirit"), but rather solidarity ("I have concerns about so and so who is a deeply disturbed psychopath").

There is both a practical and psychological reason for not including third parties at this point in the process. The practical reason is control of the information. The more we open the conflict for others to discuss, the more difficult it is to manage the conflict. The psychological reason relates to the issue of solidarity. The first thing I selfishly want and tell myself I need in a disagreement is someone to agree with me. For years, I have listened to folks explain how they needed to share the conflict with their prayer partner or accountability friend, when in actuality, they just needed validation or more input to strengthen their argument before going to the other person.

While all the steps are important, this step and the next are the most explosive if they are not handled privately and gracefully.

V. THE SENSITIVITY STEP—"IN PRIVATE DISCUSS"

Step five maintains that we must approach the other person personally and sensitively, which means privately. The setting is private because, depending on the nature of the conflict and the amount of information already identified between the two people, privacy allows for the best possible outcome.

This might seem an odd place to share a story about the nation's most famous solo sailor but stay with me. I have been fascinated by the story of Michael Plant since first reading "Mystery at Sea" in a *Sports Illustrated* article in 1992. My recent reading of the book, *Coyote Lost at Sea*, by Julia Plant, Michael's sister, has only heightened my interest.[63] These are the basics of this mysterious story.

Despite a number of obstacles, Michael makes the decision in the autumn of 1992 to compete in the Vendee Globe Challenge, a nonstop solo sailboat race around the world. He scrambles for sponsors right up until race time. His new racing yacht named *Coyote*, is a 60-foot,

21,500-pound fiberglass lightweight capable of ripping through the seas at 25 knots.

Plant runs into trouble almost as soon as he leaves New York City. He loses all electrical power around October 19, his fourth day at sea, and no one hears from Plant again until October 21, when he contacts a passing freighter via his battery-operated VHF radio. He says, "I have no power, but I'm working on the problem." He ends the transmission with a message: "Tell Helen (his fiancée) not to worry." It is Plant's last direct communication. Onshore computers identify a faint distress signal from his emergency beacon on October 27.

On Nov. 22, a Greek tanker spots Plant's $650,000 racing boat, *Coyote*, which has been missing at sea for 32 days, 460 miles north of the Azores, off the coast of Portugal. *Coyote* is floating upside down; its mast, knifing 85 feet into the freezing water, is still rigged. The boat's hull is in one piece. The day before Thanksgiving, divers from the French tug Malabar are able to inspect the high-tech boat's four water-tight compartments. They find the *Coyote's* life raft, half inflated, in the cockpit, but they do not find Plant. What they do find out is this.

The *Coyote* is intact, mast with sails, complete hull and twin rudders, except for the carbon fiber keel. The 8,400-pound keel bulb is gone and without this to provide counterweight, the boat could not stay upright.

Also, inexplicably, Plant, an experienced sailor, who has sailed around the world three times, fails to register his battery powered Raytheon 406 EPIRB (Emergency Position-Indicating Radio Beacon) transmitter before sailing, which means that computers are unable to relay the information to coastal officials.

Buried in the cold, harsh reality of this story are two principles that speak not only to solo sailors, but also to those who are willing to move into the deep waters of a private conflict resolution.

Principle one is there must be more weight below the waterline than above. In a relationship, more weight below the waterline than above speaks to the need for offering the gift every relationship needs to start with, the benefit of doubt. If each person can enter this private discussion offering the other person the benefit of doubt, the chance of this relationship remaining upright and sailing ahead will significantly increase.

Principle two refers to the fact that we must always be willing to register our need for help, even before we need it. In other words, if we enter into a private conversation about conflict in a relationship, it will not only demonstrate our desire and value for this particular relationship, we will also establish a pattern of being vulnerable that enriches and empowers relationships.

VI. THE PROBLEM STEP—"THE PROBLEM"

All the previous steps have led us to this, the step that actually deals with the problem. No wonder people tire of the journey to living in reconciled relationships. However, those who regularly and redemptively make this journey, not only say the journey is worth it, but also remind us that not to reconcile brings unbearable pain. Veterans of this journey know that the actual problem is not what lingers in our memories. What lingers are the changes that take place in the hearts of the rare breed of people who develop **Stay in the Room** relationships.

A case in point comes from a cartoon character from my youth. Popeye, the Sailor Man, made his first public appearance on January 17, 1929 and remains one of the most widely recognized and best-loved cartoon personalities. Matter of fact, it is mind-boggling, but true, that one of his cartoons airs somewhere in the world nearly every minute of every day!

Popeye is short, balding and ugly by anyone's standards. He is cast as the underdog with a long fuse and a keen sense of fair play who invites empathy when he says, "That's all I can stands, and I can't stands no more!"

Originally created for the comic book medium, Popeye makes his jump to the silver screen in a 1933 Betty Boop cartoon. Nearly 600 cartoons are made and are still in worldwide syndication.

What I most remember about him, however, is what he says whenever he makes a mistake or feels inadequate. He would always say the same thing: "I yam what I yam." Not given to complexity, Popeye is a simple, pipe-smoking, tattoo-wearing sailor man, who knows to set reasonable expectations. Clearly, his expectations are unpretentious. "I yam what I yam and that's all that I yam."

While I am encouraged by his willingness to admit his humanity, I am also challenged by his passivity to accept his fate. Are we simply the sum total of our gene pool and environmental experiences? Is it possible for a man or a woman (and in this case, a cartoon character) to be more than "I yam what I yam and that's all that I yam?"

I refer to Popeye as we move to the problem step for two reasons. First, his willingness to lean into his humanity and minimize expectations are worthy goals for discussing relational differences. Conflict has a way of igniting our defensive mechanisms long before we have heard the "walk a mile in my shoes" story of the other person. Coming as you "yam" rather than arriving with a briefcase of defense documents will provide an excellent start to discussing the problem.

Second, however lovable Popeye's humanity is in its persistent simplicity, he cannot expect to participate in the dynamic of relational conflict and be the same person. When two people enter into an exchange of divergent views that are always personal and perplexing, and the goal of that exchange is reconciliation (we discuss that next), both parties will likely be a better version of themselves, more than "that's all I yam."

When the Bible says we are only "a little lower than the angels" (Psalm 8: 5), and that "if any person is in Christ, he or she is a new creature; the old things have passed away; the new things have come" (II Corinthians 5: 17), then I have to believe living in redemptively reconciled relationships will not allow me to be "what I yam and that's all that I yam."

We can be humored by Popeye's predicaments and inspired by his vulnerability, but please, do not let this cartoon man tell you all is fixed and fated by who we "yam." No, we can be more. We can be better. We can be transformed, slowly, but steadily by the grace of God as we live in **Stay in the Room** relationships.

VII. THE RECONCILIATION STEP—
"FOR THE PURPOSE OF RECONCILIATION"

Let me begin with the most important statement of this whole chapter: confrontation is only good when reconciliation is the goal! If this is the most important statement of the whole chapter, then this is the most important question for accomplishing step seven: "Do I want to be right or redemptive?"

All steps lead to the purpose of reconciliation. From a definition standpoint, reconciliation is simply a restoration of relations. It consists of "the action of making one view or belief compatible with another."[64] The root word, conciliation, refers to the action of stopping someone from being angry.

So, what is reconciliation? Reconciliation is a decision within a broken relationship to reach a place of mercy and understanding rather than declaring a winner and loser. This does not mean, however, that there will not be some blame accepted or some responsibility assumed.

For our purposes, it is important to know what reconciliation is not. Reconciliation is not easy. Reconciliation is not pretty. Reconciliation is not happily ever after. In other words, reconciliation is not resolution. Most of the reconciliation I experience does not bring a resolve of all the irritating and disagreeable issues. It brings peace of mind, in that biblical guidelines were followed and obedience to God was pursued.

Keith Larson tells the story of a young, husky 13-year-old farm boy who is very ambitious. He works from dawn to dusk, and his parents are extremely proud of him. For the boy's 14th birthday, his father buys him a secondhand Gravely mowing tractor. The Gravely Company makes exceptional tractors, and the boy is thrilled. He begins to earn extra money by mowing yards and fields for neighbors and the people in the nearby town. The young man takes flawless care of his machine; he washes and cleans the motor and even shines the exterior.

One day he notices the blade is dull. The teenager cautiously drives the tractor into the barn and turns it over to remove the bolt on the blade. Having been around machinery his whole life, he knows to loosen a bolt by turning it counterclockwise. He puts a hefty wrench on the bolt and gives it a turn. It only slightly moves, and then it doesn't budge.

This young man is proud of his physical strength. He is a star lineman on the school football team. But he can't move that bolt at all, and he already decides not to bother his father for help on such a routine matter.

Just then he remembers what his father told him in a similar situation. Get a longer piece of pipe and put it over the wrench handle to get some leverage. So, he gets a pipe and places it over the handle.

Next, he pulls on the pipe. Nothing. He gets under the pipe with his back and tries to lift it, but the bolt does not move. Finally, in humiliation, the young man loads the tractor into the family pickup to the Gravely dealer in town.

When he gets there, the mechanic examines the stuck bolt and says, "Wait a minute. Let me check something." He takes the model number and does some research. When he returns, he says, "I hate to tell you this, but for several years the Gravely Company reversed the threads on that bolt. You have been tightening that sucker trying to loosen it. And don't worry about being strong, son. You've tightened it so soundly, we are going to have to burn it off with a torch."[65]

Yes, I recognize this is a story about a relationship between a man and his machine, but I also know it is instructive for our discussion of reconciliation as well.

This story has all the elements of most relationships needing reconciliation. A person is well intended and rewarded for being a hard worker. He is even proud of his strength and consistency in doing his job. But the relationship he has with his machine goes awry. It is frustrating and confusing.

He does everything he knows to do and trusts that his previous knowledge in his relationship with this machine (everyone knows you turn a bolt counterclockwise to loosen it) will provide the needed solution. When it doesn't, he doubles down. He presses and pushes and resists getting help until the relationship is at a standstill.

The help he needs comes from some personal and albeit surprising information that he receives (not from the machine because, of course, it can't talk), but from those closest to the machine who can speak for it, the manufacturers. Sadly, the delay in going to the manufacturers resulted in significantly more damage to the machine and to the other person in the relationship.

One other point will assist with this parallel. I chose this story between man and machine, not to be cute, but to be accurate. More often than not, one of the people in a dispute resembles a machine. They do not feel deeply. They have lived a simple, repetitive life. They do not like change or conflict so they will likely resist coming to deal with conflict. That would likely mean opening up not only about how they feel, but also revealing something about them that few people know.

Think about it, but do not use it as the opening story for your next reconciliation meeting, especially if you identify the other person as the hard-to-turn bolt with no personality!

A Story of an Oil Change on the Way to Life Change

The day is littered with anticipation. I am planning to meet three of my closest friends in Louisville, Kentucky. It is the yearly gathering of a foursome of guys who trained in karate with me while I was a seminary student.

I do not remember when I first felt the urge to measure my manhood by changing the oil in my car. Being mechanically dysfunctional, I generally left anything needing tools to someone else.

Nevertheless, I pull out the small tool kit and quickly change the oil in my Honda Accord. I finish with a manly sigh and back out of the garage, excited for a workout followed by a night of manly bonding.

Easing onto the expressway and clicking on my cruise control, I smile with a sense of accomplishment. It is only minutes before I see the idiot light begin to flash on my dashboard. I call it such because my brother, who was the mechanic in our family, used to warn me that if a light flashes on your dash, you are an idiot if you don't stop and discover the problem.

I pull to the side of the road and release the hood latch. I raise the hood and begin my clueless journey to determine what is wrong. The engine is still there, and it is running, so I decide to continue my journey. It did not last long. Within a mile or two, the car sputters to an unceremonious stop. I hear my brother's voice say, "It is called an idiot light for a reason!"

I begin my mercy calls, hoping to play innocent, all the while knowing, my last-minute oil change must have something to do with my abbreviated trip to Louisville. I call my contact at a local garage and then AAA. The car is picked up. I call a friend to come and get me when I arrive at the garage. It seems like only minutes before the mechanic calls to tell me I will need a new engine. He mentions that the oil filter is the culprit. For some reason, it did not seal properly the last time the oil was changed, and all the oil leaked out of the car. Important note: oil leaks out the bottom of the engine when the issue is an oil filter!

I borrow a car to finish my trip, hoping to bury my grief and stupidity for a few hours. When I return, I discover a group of mechanics from my church had towed my car to their home and began a restoration project of unforgettable proportions. They use all their resources and some others from the church to locate an engine for a very reasonable price. In a matter of days, my engine is replaced, and I am presented with a unique award in front of the whole congregation. It is a wooden plague that can be purchased from any trophy shop, but it is the burned piston attached to it that makes it unforgettable. The small gold engraving next to the piston quotes a Bible verse: "they came together with one accord." (Remember, my car was a Honda Accord.)

The moral of my Honda experience is simple: mechanical dysfunction leads to mechanical breakdown and unless rescued by friends who offer mercy and mechanical expertise, the cost will be severe and the experience overwhelming.

Becoming vulnerable is sometimes learned the hard way. Whether it is allowing yourself to parasail two hundred feet in the air and learning to let go sooner, or allowing your pride to be reduced through compromise, the journey toward a relationship that is whole and even joyful is always worth the risk.

4

Discernment: "What do I do when I don't know what to do?"

DISCERNMENT: MIND TRAINING FOR PERSPECTIVE

"You can get all As and still flunk life."[66]

Walker Percy

HERE IS A story I have relived many, many, many times. It is a story that takes place on a fateful night in the summer of 1975. Two men come out of the house next to mine at 44th Street and Decoursey Avenue in Covington, Kentucky. My mother, my older brother, Buddy, and I stand on the front porch, having just arrived from our separate evening activities. Buddy, as he often does, stops to check-in on family happenings, ever the social beast. A friendly gathering of inconsequential intentions becomes a murderous night of lost hopes and wasted promises.

While walking toward their car on the street in front of our home, two men from the neighboring house suddenly pause, their gaze foreboding. Even after decades of reflection on that night, I struggle to know why they choose to linger in our direction. My best is a drug-infested anger over having the police called on them earlier in the evening over loud music. While that complaint did not originate with us, we become the object of their scorn.

Pulling a gun, they wave it menacingly. Taking the lead, I tell them we do not want any trouble. They move toward their car when suddenly all hell breaks loose. I am 15-20 feet away when the first bullet penetrates my right lung, knocking me to the ground, not so much from the force of the bullet, but the trauma of the wound in my chest and loss of blood. I pass out amid screams and more gunshots.

Sirens wake me from the nightmare, and I am led to a police cruiser, as my brother is loaded into an ambulance. All the way to the hospital, I cling to life, the wind from the lowered window becoming a lifeline. I stay conscious even though the hole in my chest is burning with each fragile breath.

Two brothers are rushed into adjourning rooms in the emergency room of St. Elizabeth Hospital and I soon hear the nurse say words no brother should ever have to hear: "The other one didn't make it."

My life over the next few days is a swirl of excruciating pain. A chest tube is hammered between my ribs to expand my collapsed lung. I take regular trips to the beach of my fantasies through demurral-induced dreams. Back massages from a large African American nurse become my solace in the night as I ache to forget the darkness.

I remain in the Intensive Care Unit for six days. In between blurred consciousness and unforgettable pain, I have two main visitors. One is my mother, the other is Neva, a young lady I have been dating for eight months. Not surprisingly, my mother is frozen in the utter agony of the death of her first-born son. Her visits represent hard realities I resist facing.

To my surprise, my petite brunette girlfriend, with a high-pitched voice and sunny personality, becomes my tunnel through the fog. Her gentle, tireless presence draws me from my pain with an effervescent anticipation for another day. Slowly, she awakens me to the possibility of tomorrow.

The seventh day of my hospital stay brings a move to a private room, where I encounter the ghost of vengeance and death. Having trained in karate for decades of my life, I secretly plan to take the murderer's life with simple planning and pinpoint execution. The problem is I would likely be identified. "Black belt karate instructor carries out revenge on brother's killer" would be a likely headline in the newspaper.

I imagine a plot to eradicate the killer with a gun and then dispense with the evidence. As I lose consciousness for the night, those are my last thoughts. Then comes the dream . . . or was it? While I am uncertain of the exact nature of the communication, I am crystal clear about the message. Imagining my exacting of revenge, I hear a voice say, "I thought you gave your life to Me. If you kill him, you give your life to death. Which is it going to be?"

One day in my private room and I make it through the most discerning moment of my life. I am released a day later from the hospital, but in reality, I am released the moment I hear, believe, and begin to live the truth about giving my future to life. I am released to forever remember the power of discernment when life and death hang in the balance.

Discernment—A Door That Opens the Truth

Discernment is the ability to detect, to recognize and to perceive what is happening. It is insight beyond the obvious and outside the realm of facts. In summary, discerning people have more than knowledge and insight. They have understanding and perspective. Discerning people move beyond their wants to their needs. Discerning people make the right choices amid tough circumstances.

Spiritually speaking, discernment enters the realm of wisdom. King Solomon prayed for such wisdom: "So give Thy servant an understanding heart to judge Thy people to discern between good and evil . . ." (I Kings 3:9). The Apostle Paul said, "And this I pray, that your love may abound still more and more in real knowledge and all discernment" (Philippians 1:9).

What problem, relationship or situation is stirring in your life today that needs a word of discernment? The answer is not likely to come in a nighttime dream or even the voice of a spiritual prompting, but believe me when I tell you, it will come.

It may come in the word of a friend, the admonishment of a doctor or counselor, or maybe in a cautioning from God through one of his followers. Discernment will come when you honestly seek it, genuinely want it, and wholehearted act on it.

After decades of counseling and coaching people seeking discernment about issues in their lives, I am convinced that given time to understand an issue, people usually know what to do. What they lack, however, is the courage to act and the willingness to let someone walk with them as they make critical decisions. Discernment opens the door, giving courage to make tough, life transforming choices.

Discernment—A Process for Decision-Making

Literally, to discern means "to distinguish, judge, and make decisions."[67] Practically speaking, discernment is more challenging to accomplish than to define. Our goal in this chapter is to identify a discernment process for relational decision-making.

Even though I have identified seven steps in this discernment process, and they appear separate and distinct, discernment is more ART than SCIENCE. Also, while these steps can be accomplished with the input of only one party, the healthier, more mature relationships operate with the input of both parties.

I. DETERMINE THE NATURE OF THE RELATIONSHIP.

Many times, a relationship fails for no other reason than different perspectives of the relationship.

- One person sees an acquaintance, the other person sees a friend.
- One sees a short-term relationship; the other sees a long-lasting relationship.
- One participant wants to get something from the relationship; the other needs to give something to the relationship.

These different expectations can be identified when considering the difference between a contract and a covenant. Generally speaking, a contract is a legal term given in a logical and fair agreement between equals who are mutually dependent on their understanding of that arrangement.

Just as the word contract is generally used in a legal context, the word covenant is most often used in a Biblical or spiritual context. A covenant relationship is identified as one between God and man as well as those united in a marriage relationship. Given that distinction, a covenant is a Biblical term given to a loving and loyal agreement between unequals. My point is not one of being unequal in gifts or abilities, but unequal in basic nature. Just as God is unequal to human beings in nature, men and women are unequal or different in their natures and identities as males and females. However, while a covenant relationship is one among unequals, it thrives on the belief that these unequal parties are mutually submissive in their desire for love and community.

While the difference between contracts and covenants may seem cavernous, I believe, especially for the follower of Christ, these differences are more levels of maturation than descriptions of limitation. Every relationship starts with characteristics of a contract and depending on the time, development and maturation of the relationship, it will remain a contract or it will by the nature of the relationship be drawn into something more.

While I certainly understand the Biblical characterization of marriage relationships being covenants, I think many of those same characteristics exist and empower other relationships. The difference is not a description of two separate entities, but a continuum of how the nature of a relationship develops and grows.

Lou, the Auto Man

Let me offer an example. I have a contract relationship with Lou, the man who takes care of my car at his automotive repair shop. I, regularly and routinely, enter into an extension of our unofficial but ongoing contract for repair and maintenance of my car. I agree to pay him for services rendered and outside of minor issues of schedule and the securing of needed parts, our contract remains agreeable and satisfying.

Imagine if Lou's wife or family member dies and I discover he does not have a church or a close relationship to a minister who can handle the funeral service for his loved one. What if Lou asks me for help in this crisis? Do I pull out a "cost for services rendered" contract or do I lean into the hope that this relationship might be moving from a contract to a covenant?

The answer is obvious and should that happen, no matter how many other times I re-enter my contract with Lou to repair my car, the relationship will live, thrive and grow in the nature of a covenant relationship because covenants are the deeper, wider and richer forms of relationships.

When we determine the nature of a relationship under question, we move to the expectation stage.

II. DISCOVER THE <u>EXPECTATION</u> OF THE RELATIONSHIP.

Once the nature of a relationship is identified, attention must be devoted to expectations. Sadly, we can experience the delicate and difficult side of expectations long before we even realize they exist. Case in point is a story experienced by my social butterfly granddaughter, Jensen.

This preschooler sees her friends from school at a neighborhood park, only to discover what she expects is not what she gets. She expects them to recognize and include her into their playtime fun. They did not expect to see her outside of school, as they had come with other family and friends. They run off to an isolated part of the playground, two friends clinging to their newfound feelings of togetherness at the expense of a little girl whose expectations are crushed. It will be many years before Jensen can define and understand expectations, but that does not protect her from the confusion and hurt when she discovers her name missing from her friend's exclusive club list.

In Tonya Hurley's novel, *Homecoming*, she offers an important distinction on expectations: "If you expect nothing, you can never be disappointed. Apart from a few starry-eyed poets or monks living on a mountaintop somewhere, however, we all have expectations. We not only have them, we need them. They fuel our dreams, our hopes, and our lives like some super-caffeinated energy drink."[68]

Expectations are not optional; they are real, ongoing and necessary. However, what we do with them and how we allow them to shape us, will determine an important step in all our relationships. Stephen R. Covey, in his classic, *The 7 Habits of Highly Effective People*, offers a powerful perspective on the relational component of expectations: "Treat a man as he is and he will remain as he is. Treat a man as he can and should be and he will become as he can and should be."[69]

Since relationships have an important role in establishing expectations, vibrant, healthy relationships regularly clarify and communicate expectations.

National Public Radio ran a story a few years ago (August 22, 2010) on their *All Things Considered* broadcast. Entitled *No More Gym? Don't Worry, Your Muscles Remember,* it explains how new research shows that strength training not only builds muscle, it also produces new muscle nuclei which remain when the muscle mass goes away.[70] In other words, if a person works out and builds muscle and then stops, the nuclei of the muscle remains and if a physical regimen resumes, these nuclei give a head start to the return of the muscle mass to its past strength level.

For our purpose in understanding the role of expectations in relationships, it is imperative to understand that not only do muscles have memories, but expectations also have memories and therein lies both the power and delicacy of our expectations. Expectations, like muscles, have a nuclei of hope based on the emotional strength developed from years of investing in what C. R. Synder identifies as "agency and pathways."

In his book, *The Psychology of Hope,* the late Dr. Synder of the University of Kansas, moves hope from a simple aspiration to a purposeful process.

For him, hope is not simply an emotion, but rather a thought process of *goals* (expectations), *pathways* (plans), *agency* (energy) and *barriers* (resistance). Hope happens when a person sets goals, has the tenacity to pursue those goals, believes in their abilities to accomplish those goals and accounts for the barriers that can block the attainment of those goals.[71]

Can you remember a moment in your life when your expectations were crushed because you either did not have a reasoned plan or the energy for the expected goal was spent on other endeavors which ultimately ended in an unhappy outcome? Have you ever hoped for a nice steak dinner and ended up having a sandwich? How about a night of intimacy planned with your spouse that was interrupted by friends who have no boundaries? Or perhaps worst of all, you had planned a public marriage proposal that backfired in the worst possible way? The key to our hope is not fragile emotion, but sustaining memory.

To use our previous story on muscle memory, the nuclei or hope within our emotions is strengthened each time goals are set, pursued, attained or blocked. So, just as muscles have memories, expectations have memories and the hope health of our memories will directly impact our ability to discover the expectations needed for each relationship.

Millvina, the Dream Baby

She is only two months old when she is wrapped in a sack and lowered into a lifeboat on the freezing North Atlantic Ocean. Millvina Dean is a participant in a dark night of history. She died a few years ago at the age of 97, the last survivor of the 1912 sinking of the RMS Titanic.

We all know the basics of that fearfully fated night. Sailing on a placid sea, the Royal Mail Steamer Titanic is dubbed unsinkable by pundits of modern technology. She is the largest moving object in the world, a floating city 882.5 feet long and 93 feet wide weighing 103,774,720 pounds. Much is written about the pride of the builders, the scarcity of lifeboats (enough for about half of the 2200 plus passengers) and the glaring discrepancy between survival rates of the first-versus third-cabin passengers.

Millvina Dean dies where she lived all her life, Southampton, England. That does not seem unusual given the lack of transience for her generation compared to those living in postmodern times. It does not seem unusual until you read it is "from this city" her family boarded the Titanic's voyage to America.

If you read further, you discover the rest of the story. Her father sells his pub and hopes (there is that word again) to open a tobacco shop in Kansas City, Missouri where his wife has relatives. Millvina's mother, Georgette, also among the 706 survivors, later tells how her husband saves his family by quickly moving his loved ones out of third-cabin quarters.

I wonder about the dream. Did her mother return to England after the tragedy and grieve not only her husband's death, but also his dream to go to America? While we don't know details of what happens to the family, Millvina, for some reason, decides to stay in her homeland. I cannot help but wonder about her Dad's lost dream.[72]

So, if the nuclei or hope of our emotions is strengthened each time goals are set, pursued, attained or blocked by a barrier which results in either the loss of that goal or the re-routing of that goal to yet another goal, then are we to conclude that Millvina and or her mother were simply unable to recover the sunken dream of the family leader? In their journey to manage their loss, the nuclei of their emotions did not contain the experiences necessary to continue the dream of going on to America.

What is frightening about this example is that people do not even have to be alive for us to understand the importance of negotiating healthy expectations for relationships past and present. My sense for this story is that the emotional nuclei of the family partriarch's dream never translated into the hope health of either Millvina or her mother. It is easier to rediscover their expectations for their loss by going back home rather than moving forward into an even more uncertain world.

Discovering the nuclei or hope of each of our relationships comes when we determine the nature and discover the expectation for that relationship. Then and only then will we be able to design a mutually satisfying **Stay in the Room** relationship.

III. DESIGN A STRATEGY FOR THE RELATIONSHIP.

Based on this understanding of the nature and expectation of the relationship, how then will we design a strategy that appropriately expresses our values, which will guide and guard any relationship?

Let me first offer a sad, sobering fact about most relationships. Most never reach the strategy stage because it simply takes too much time, effort and barefaced honesty. This step is the "rubber meets the road" phase for discerning the destination of a particular relationship. Assuming the nature of your bond is identified, and the expectation of the relationship is reasonable, now how will we design a strategy for it?

Pain, the Purpose Plan

I receive a call from the nurse who puts me on hold for the doctor. Quickly moving from polite greeting to nitty-gritty truth, he exudes an air of absolute confidence about the test results. While this quest for information was a circuitous journey into the mystery of medical knowledge, the results are now at a no-brainer, dead-end conclusion.

Couched in a barrage of medical terminology, the doctor says, "We are going to have to go in there and repair that thing." "That thing" is a bone resting on a nerve at the sixth vertebrae; those vital bone connectors provide the housing structure needed for the sense-system of our bodies, better known as the central nervous system.

I greet his words with relieved regret. I am relieved to have a treatable problem, but regretful the solution includes the word surgery, an experience that includes incisions and staples and a significant dose of good old-fashioned PAIN. If only I had known!

I seek a second opinion. Test results in hand, I walk into the office of a highly recommended neurosurgeon. I find myself recording every sound and movement in the waiting room. Everyday conversations become my obsession. I need to hear what they are saying about this yet unknown man with a scalpel.

A kind of wizard behind the curtain, I listen for their stories of how he takes weakness and gives strength. I record the movement of the wizard's helpers. Are they just doing a job or are they true disciples of

this healing man? Are they collecting a paycheck or are they partici-
pating in a larger plan? My answers come soon.

I am invited into a small room and told to put on one of those pride-re-
ducing, peekaboo gowns. I do so, dutifully, and await the wizard. I hear
his voice outside the room. It seems nice. Then he arrives, a bit shorter
than I have imagined. Following a reassuring smile, he begins a brief
examination. Poking here and prodding there, his demeanor offers no
clues except for his thoroughness. Rolling around the room on a small
stool, I am impressed with his dexterity. He operates well with both feet.
I am looking for any sign of competence!

His conclusions bring back that feeling of relieved regret, but
somehow different this time. Perhaps hearing it for the second time, and
hearing it in person, cements my reality. He takes out a booklet, similar
in size to a comic book, with the title *Cervical Disk Surgery* emblazoned
across the top. Methodically, he begins his diagnostic deliberations.

With words like "stenosis" and "degenerative disk disease," he circles
the appropriate pictures and slowly makes his way to the obvious. I need
a lumbar disc laminectomy to correct this problem.

He further explains that while this is fairly minor surgery, it is
still neurosurgery and can result in catastrophic paralysis like that of
Christopher Reeves. Nothing like name-dropping to throw you head-
first into the frightening world of reality! For the first time, I realize
that surgery is not only about relieving pain (that has no purpose); it is
also about causing pain (that has purpose). It is about trading one kind
of pain for another. It is about risk and hope. It is about life and death!

Then comes an oddly humorous moment that would later bear the
bitter fruit of reality. He says, "This is really fun surgery because you will
get almost immediate relief, although you will hate me for the post-surgery neck pain." We chuckle and with that I make my decision to do
this. This began our journey into the world of paperwork, scheduling,
gowns, drugs, more drugs and yes, PAIN—both the disappearance of
the old and the discovery of the new.

This experience demonstrates a strategy for relationships:

- First, <u>a decision to trust</u> another person is based on information gathered in the nature and expectation steps of the relationship. Relationships are primarily about trust, whether it is a friend to whom you entrust your heart or a doctor to whom you entrust your healing.

When was the last time you were hurt or disappointed with a relationship? How difficult was it to begin to trust that person again? Maybe you never did. Did it impact your feelings when a new relationship began to bloom, or cause a level of suspicion that surfaced on other relationships? Depending on the length and depth of the disappointment, recognize hesitation to trust again is real.

- Second, there is <u>an acceptance of pain</u> as a part of the process for long-term health. Any strategy for healthy bodies and relationships will include the acknowledgement of some reasonable amount of pain.

I recently witnessed the resurrection of an old and distant friendship caused by a boatload of disappointment. We lost touch due to our sanctified certainties. I suspect you know how that goes. Suddenly, paths aren't crossed due to discomfort. Before you know it, weeks become months, months become years, and words are rarely, if ever, spoken.

Until one day, a window, or perhaps a peephole of opportunity appears. It is born through social media; my comment reached him through one of his children. After some clarification, he asked me to call. I did and he simply said, "I'm sorry." He was not speaking about the past, just the intention regarding the social media post, but in my heart, it was all the same. Those simple, sacred, long overdue words had broken the pain of our past and revived our desire to move to a better place. Now, I text him periodically and he addresses me as "my friend." And so it is for those of us who are willing to accept our pain and perhaps even trade it for something better, renewed friendship.

- Third, there is an <u>intentional plan</u> to know and understand the person trusted with a significant portion of one's physical (in the case of surgery) or emotional (in the case of **Stay in the Room** relationships) health.

One might ask the question: How long does it take to know and understand someone? The answer depends on age, maturity, and desire of the parties involved. For example, lengthy courtships allow couples to see one another in varied situations; i.e. times of grief, struggle, victory, change. As I alluded to earlier, it was during the shooting and loss of my brother that I knew my relationship with Neva had the depth and strength for a solid future. Lengthy courtships also allow couples to pay attention to how someone spends money and what holds priority for their time. It allows one to witness spiritual depth and baggage from the family of origin. When making decisions for a lifetime, let time be your friend and counsel.

My theory about **Stay in the Room** relationships is built on the premise that all relationships are valuable and all people are redeemable. It does not mean all relationships are the same, which is emotionally impossible. It does mean that no one, absolutely no one, is outside the room of relationships.

Reflecting on the graph from earlier in the book, some relationship partners may be in the corner of hurt, fear, blame, or even vengeance, but my hope for ALL relationships is we will ALWAYS know that together, we can find a way to the table of reconciliation. Experience tells me many relationships never make it to that table because of an unwillingness of one or both parties to walk through the strategies featured in this book. We must make the decision to trust the future and whatever part we played in the pain of our past.

- Fourth, there is an ongoing <u>assessment of "relieved regret."</u>

In surgery, as well as everyday relationships, we expect some level of regret for the upcoming pain, but also hope for the eventual relief that results from the scalpel of the surgeon or **Staying in the Room** with any and all who desire relational health. The relief found in surgery and relationships is about valuing pain, risk, hope, and endurance.

I am convinced that these four steps can be the building blocks for designing a strategy for all relationships

IV. ADOPT AN ATTITUDE OF <u>COLLABORATION.</u>

Antisthenes, the Greek philosopher and pupil of Socrates, offers a nuanced way to view the idea of collaboration: "There are only two people who can tell you the truth about yourself; an enemy who has lost his temper and a friend who loves you dearly."[73] The philosopher recognizes that the vehicle for hearing the truth is not a one-way conversation with friends, but a broader collaboration with the disagreements of our enemies.

Let's examine the difference between cooperation and collaboration.

Consider this exaggerated premise: we cooperate with friends and we collaborate with enemies. The implication is operating with our friends can be meaningful, but laboring with those we do not consider friends can be disappointing.

What if we chose to labor (until something is born) with those who are different and often disagreeable? This means we lower the level of competition (where we prove we are right) and we raise the level of purpose (where we trade being right for being redemptive).

Let's simplify with this clarifying qualifier: This whole idea about collaborating with our enemies, or simply those with whom we have significant disagreement, can be confusing. I do not mean spending inordinate amounts of time and energy trying to make our enemies into our friends. What I do mean is that we never stop listening to our critics and we never stop laboring with points of disagreement. **Stay in the Room** relationships stay open to the piece of truth in our differences and utilizes it as a starting point for some level of collaboration.

I grew up watching my Hazard, Kentucky, coal-miner grandfather we lovingly called "Dadi" sharpen his pocketknife on a whetstone. No wonder I was confused when I read the oft-quoted proverb, "Iron sharpens iron, so one person sharpens another" (Proverbs 27:16).

He taught me the only way to sharpen an iron blade was to use a tool with a different edge or texture. Biblical interpreters usually compare the "Iron sharpens iron" part of the verse with two similarly strong people, however, this verse actually does not promote uniformity. If resistance sharpens a blade, then a similarly smooth blade will not work. The iron that sharpens iron must be an entirely different tool. Might this also speak to the need for the collaboration of enemies?

A Tale of Lost Limbs and Found Lives

This is a tale of an orphan and a marine, born over 5,000 miles apart, who find each other because of what they have lost.

Oksana Alexandrovna Boudarchuk is born in Khmelnitsky, Ukraine on June 19, 1989 with six toes, five webbed fingers on each hand, and no thumbs, a condition called tibial hemimelia. One leg is six inches shorter and both legs are missing weight-bearing bones. Her parents go missing in action and she begins a lonely and catastrophic journey through revolving orphanage doors. She is beaten and raped with regularity.

A single woman and speech pathology professor, Gay Master from Buffalo, New York, begins her search for a newborn baby to adopt. When someone shows her a picture of Oksana, she declares, "That's my child." After persevering the two-year ban on Ukrainian adoptions, her dream is finally realized. On a late night in January of 1997, Gay finds eight-year-old Oksana wrapped in a sweater in a freezing building. When she wakes up she says in Ukrainian, "I know who you are. You're my mother. I have a picture."

Oksana and Gay move to Louisville, Kentucky in 2001. It feels like an avalanche of change for the now budding teenager. After securing prosthetic legs, Oksana is introduced to the sport of rowing. She enjys the privacy. As she attacks the water, "the central theme of her early life was inverted. She could be as violent as she wanted, while everything around her stayed serene."

Rob Jones grows up on a 200-acre farm in Lovettsville, Virginia. During his junior year at Virginia Tech University, he makes the decision that will change his life forever. He signs up for the Marines. Without strong political or moral reasons or even a full understanding of why his country is at war in Iraq and Afghanistan, he decides to serve.

In January of 2008, Rob goes to Iraq as a lance corporal specializing in IED (improvised explosive device) detection. In April of 2010, he is deployed to Afghanistan. One day in July, while clearing the area after a blasting cap explodes, an IED destroys his legs. After a morphine injection, he flies to his base, then Germany, and finally back to the states at Bethesda Naval Hospital.

I discover what brings this marine and orphan together when I read their amazing story in a *Sports Illustrated* article by Michael Rosenberg in 2012.[74] Oksana and Rob are training for the Paralympics in London in mixed double sculls. A double scull is a two-person rowing boat equipped with two oars, one in each hand that is used in the sport of competitive rowing. They win a bronze medal, the first U.S. medal ever in this event.

What an odd story of collaboration! Think about the circumstances and choices that eventually bring them together.

The common denominators are loss and pain . . . loss of limbs and use of pain to heighten their awareness of life's fragile nature. Both know that expectations and realities must be negotiated and renewed, or life will disappear.

What eventually spurs them into action is the belief that they will not waste a single day of their lives. And neither should we!

The fact is we are all wounded warriors in our relationships. No matter how perfect and protected our lives may seem, none of us is immune to the loss and pain of relational disappointment. With each disappointment, like Oskana and Rob, we have the choice to numb and isolate from the pain or to engage and be empowered by it. We have the choice to say, "I will reduce my exposure to relational pain and loss" or "I will re-invest my pain for relational growth and maturity, thus modeling the power of collaboration."

Collaboration is defined as the desire to "work jointly on an activity, especially in an intellectual endeavor."[75] If we honestly desire vibrant and healthy relationships, we must be willing to allow our best and our worst, our easiest and most challenging, our thriving and our most debilitating relationships to work jointly on an activity that produces or creates something better.

Decades of being in the trenches with people trying to discern their way through dysfunctional or damaged relationships, reminds me that this process is most often derailed by a simple lack of humility. Many refuse to offer or even receive the gift of an apology. If collaboration is the transmission in a car that drives toward discernment, then a humble apology is the gasoline, which ignites and sustains the attitude needed to arrive at a discerning destination. **Stay in the Room** relationships demand a humble spirit.

V. BUILD AN ATMOSPHERE OF TRUST.

The deeper we move into the discernment process for **Stay in the Room** relationships, the more supernatural the journey becomes. It is not natural to embrace the humility needed to sincerely apologize. It is not natural to anticipate an atmosphere of trust once we cross the threshold of childhood maturation called "developing judgment." At an early age, we begin discerning between good and bad, trustworthy and unreliable.

Trust is defined as "assured reliance on the character, ability, strength, or truth of someone or something."[76] No wonder we tremble in the face of building an atmosphere of trust. However, it is both a daunting expectation and an absolute necessity for healthy, growing relationships. Frank Sonnenberg says as much in his book, *Follow Your Conscience*, when he declares, "Trust is like blood pressure. It's silent, vital to good health, and if abused, can be deadly."[77]

As I write this section on trust, Brene Brown's work on trust is receiving massive attention. She is a research professor at the University of Houston and author of several books. Brown deciphers seven elements of trust through the acronym, BRAVING in her book, *Rising Strong*.[78]

B – Boundaries. We have previously identified the significance of boundaries. Trust begins and ends with the establishment and acceptance of appropriate boundaries.

R – Reliability. Our earlier definition of trust began with two important words: assured reliance. Reliability is the assurance that mutually agreed upon words and actions can be reasonably aligned with expectations.

A – Accountability. We have established that "accountability is not optional for any caring, connected, growing relationship built on honest authenticity and strong boundaries." The previously mentioned need for apologizing plays a major role in accountability.

V – Vault. In order to make the BRAVING acronym work, Brown uses the word vault metaphorically. While a vault usually refers to a room or compartment reserved for the storage and safekeeping of valuables, here the writer applies it to the place where trustworthy people keep the confidential information and experiences of others.

I – Integrity. Brown's definition of integrity is "Choosing courage over comfort, choosing what's right over what's fun, fast or easy, and practicing your values, not just professing your values."

N – Non-judgment. The nature of trust implies the presence of understanding and grace. All relationships struggle, but those who persevere exhibit non-judgmental behaviors toward the honest feelings of others.

G – Generosity. The sincerity of our non-judgmental behavior will be tested and proven by the presence of generosity. Generosity in trusting relationships is expressed whenever we offer the other person the benefit of doubt. The writer says our relationship is only a trusting relationship if you can assume "the most generous interpretation possible to the intentions, words and actions of others."[79]

It is not an exaggeration to say that trust is the most important ingredient to relational decision-making. It is more important than love because love can exist without deep, valuable relationships, but deep, valuable relationships cannot exist without trust. George MacDonald said it this way: "To be trusted is a greater compliment than to be loved."[80]

A Story of Trust Forsaken

While the focus of this book is on the power and perseverance of personal relationships, the same principles apply whether they are practiced in the back bedroom of an inner-city apartment or the international waters of the Barents Sea. This is a story of trust forsaken.

I originally wrote this story on the eve of the last gasp of air for the 116 crewmembers of the Russian submarine, Kursk, trapped 354 feet below in the Barents Sea. Pending a heroic and miraculous rescue by Friday, August 18, 2000, the oxygen supply on the submarine would expire and its inhabitants would die a dark and lonely death in their 500-foot, 14,000-ton crippled vessel, which sank after an unexplained, failed military exercise the previous weekend.

I will never forget the largely silent response from Russian President Vladimir Putin who described the situation as "difficult, and I would say, critical," yet he remained on holiday in the Black Sea resort of Sochi.

I remember how every attempt to assist in the resolution of this disaster was spurned by the Russian government. An Associated Press report stated that the daily Russian newspaper, *Sevodnya*, quoted navy sources as saying Russian officers rejected all offers of help for fear of being "sacked." To clarify this, a source was quoted as saying, "Admirals for some reason think that if even one Russian sailor is saved from a Russian submarine with outside help, it certainly will end in a political catastrophe."[81]

One expert suggested that the weakening state of the submarine's occupants would likely force them to lie down in order to save energy. While I am not an expert on Russian history, I would suggest that in this particular case, the weakening state of this country's leadership, forced them to lie down in order to save face. While those resting in the damaged vessel from below assumed a posture of surrender and submission, those wrestling with the sunken ship from above adopted a posture of pride and self-sufficiency.

We would do well to learn carefully the lesson of this sad story. It is the lesson of the blinding power of pride, a pride birthed and nurtured in a cesspool of distrust and suspicion.

So, what is to be learned from this creeping shadow of lost life? Pride unleashed from humility is a powerful blindfold to the needs of others. Whether it is embarrassed countries or embattled individuals, we all need to **Stay in the Room** with each other.

VI. INSIST ON THE PRACTICE OF EMPOWERMENT.

Too often today, empowerment is a buzzword for the freedom to exercise personal power and accomplishment. In contrast, the empowerment needed for **Stay in the Room** relationships is defined by the decision to submit to being accountable and responsible to other people.

In this stage of the discernment process, all competition and control is replaced with accountability and responsibility. Competition and control start with *me*; accountability and responsibility start with *we*.

A Trip to Possibility

It sounded simple enough. My wife, Neva, points to a short, round object protruding from the florescent light under one of our kitchen cabinets. Immediately, my male hormones rise to the surface. An all-points bulletin goes out from the mechanical side of my masculinity. Of course, I know. It is a whatchamacallit that helps to power the light.

She asks if I can pull it from the light switch and get a replacement. So, I do what few mechanically dysfunctional males rarely do. I attempt the unknown. I risk rejection. I act the part. And it works. My startled surprise quickly melts into welcomed confidence. I take the test and pass. I am provider, problem-solver and Mr. Fix-it all wrapped into one.

Neva, however, is not as impressed with me as I am, as the light is still out.

Assuming that this whatchamacalilit is the cause of the problem, she asks if I can buy one at the store. I didn't need to ask what store. It is the store dreaded most by MDMs or mechanically dysfunctional males. I don't know what I hated most—their pumpkin-colored vests or their cheery how-can-we-help dispositions. Like elves of empowerment they prance their way through the store dispensing their brand of possibility.

I finally make my way through the sliding doors. I chose my time well. The crowd is low. I look for the sign that will direct me to the correct aisle and immediately see an elf of empowerment in an orange apron.

As I approach him, he nods as if he can tell I am a MDM. I show him the whatchamacallit and he does the unspeakable. Instead of getting it for me, he merely points me in a direction. I move hesitantly, hoping he will follow, but he doesn't.

So, I take the plunge. I begin the scavenger hunt, trying to match what I have in my hands with what I see on the shelves. Eventually, the numbers are identical. As I make my way to the cash register, I can't help stopping long enough to allow the non-attentive man in orange to confirm my decision. He agrees and it is like I am strolling down the aisle at a graduation ceremony. Matter of fact, I am slightly surprised the check-out attendants don't shake my hand in response to the pomp and circumstance of this momentous accomplishment.

From dysfunctional to daring in just one visit, I am suddenly empowered and if that wasn't enough, I find myself pausing at an advertisement on the way out the door. It describes upcoming Do-It-Yourself classes. What is an eyesore on the way in, now becomes . . . daresay, a possibility?

Now I am the first to admit this is a simple, exaggerated story. However, that does nothing to diminish its truth. We live isolated lives that harbor our weaknesses and inadequacies. Left to ourselves, we never see the possibility to overcome those frailties, unless someone or something draws us out and offers a reasonable opportunity to be or do more.

If you and I are in **Stay in the Room** relationships that have discernment as an active ingredient, weaknesses and inadequacies will be challenged and clarified by the regular practice of empowerment.

VII. LIVE IN LEARNING, LOVING RELATIONSHIPS.

This part of the relational discernment process for **Stay in the Room** relationships is both the most obvious and the most difficult. It is the most obvious because who doesn't want to live in loving relationships? But it is also the most difficult because many of our loving relationships are not teaching us anything. Matter of fact, many of our most loving relationships are built more on survival than learning.

Look back over the questions we address in this book and ask yourself if all these questions are actively being answered in your most significant relationships:

Authenticity: Can I really tell you who I am?

Boundaries: Can I really tell you what I need?

Compatibility: How can we get along if we are so different?

Discernment: What do I do when I don't know what to do?

If the answers to these questions is no, then I suspect your relationships are more about survival than growth. Either the people in your relationship circles do not offer you the room to ask these questions or you have grown weary from negotiating the time and effort needed to develop the answers.

The decision to intentionally live in learning, loving relationships will do one of two things. It will cause you to radically limit the number of people you allow in your relationship room, or it will force you to become vigilant in pursuing the relational "learnings" that come as a result of choosing love as the ongoing goal for all your relationships.

A Story of a Pain the the Neck

When I am finally able to wake up (control freaks hate to be put to sleep), I am immediately conscious of two things: while I feel stiff, the pain is minimal, including the right arm which had been throbbing and numb for weeks. I delay my excitement since I am clearly still drugged. Within 24 hours, I realize that 85% of the previous right arm pain is gone.

The nurses attend to my every care. They wake me up every hour on the hour to shine a flashlight in my eyes.

I find myself serendipitously energized by my post-surgery, primarily pain-free experience. It is then and there I decide I will write about this mind-boggling, body-altering experience.

The official stapler arrives with an air of quiet confidence. He smiles and says our journey into the world of necks and nerves was successful. He warns me of my Frankenstein-like neck mobility while the staples are present. I have a new and improved understanding of the phrase "a pain in the neck!"

I am then given a surprising peek behind the wizard's curtain. My surgeon, professional and reserved, leans back and listens as I express appreciation for my anesthesiologist, whom I lovingly name Dr. Poke. After listening intently, he smiles and says, "He is a good man. I have known him for a long time. Matter of fact, I had the terrible task of telling him his ten-year-old child was brain dead from a car accident a few years ago."

Stunned by both the story and the storyteller, I re-connect the pieces of my pre-surgery puzzle with Dr. Poke, the anesthesiologist. His view from behind the surgery room mask is not one etched by medical school tests and laboratory experiments. His tender presence and soft touch, now realized, is born of an agony and pain of the unforgettable kind. The awful and awkward truth about the death of his child had moved him to understand—healers heal best when they are wounded!

Pain can be the great *paralyzer* or the great *paraphraser*. It can rob us of our words and leave us in deadly silence or it can translate our stone-cold silence into words that bring life. The best part is we have a small, but crucial part in what pain accomplishes in our life.

What does this surgery story say about living in learning, loving relationships? Let me start with the obvious. There are no painless surgeries, unless it is someone else's surgery. There are no painless relationships, unless, yes, it is someone else's relationship.

If the question is how we can live in loving, learning relationships when they regularly and routinely bring pain to our lives, then the answer is found in how my anesthesiologist dealt with unspeakable relational pain in the loss of his daughter. I contend that he lived in learning, loving relationships which provided him the room to discern whether this hideous pain would act as a paralyzer or a paraphraser. His caring attention on my day of need did not portray a man frozen in an antiquated agony, but rather presented the picture of a doctor who lived, loved and learned that a healer heals best when they are wounded.

CONCLUSION

So, what do I do with a relationship when I honestly do not know what to do? My life's experience confirms that IF a person can walk through these steps, they can discover a discernment process for relational decision-making that will prove incredibly helpful and hopeful.

The facts are simple. We all deal with broken relationships. However, early in my life, I was not equipped to handle differing levels of relational dysfunction. My *modus operandi* was to analyze and argue my way to resolve relational differences. Being a decent critical thinker and quick on my wordsmithing feet, I was usually able to win most of my points. The problem came from the cost of winning.

The cost of winning a debate is high. As long as we focus on the problem and the logic of arguments and each person's ability to make a case for themselves, it resolves nothing. I began to realize something I mentioned earlier in the book: **With regard to relationships, it is always better to be redemptive than right!**

Resolution focuses on the problem, but reconciliation focuses on the relationship. Resolution wins or loses based on the logic of an argument. Reconciliation wins or loses based on the love and trust of our relationships.

Paul Scherer, American 20th century Lutheran minister and professor of homiletics at both Union and Princeton, used to say: "Faith is more like a courtship than the courtroom."[82] What he says about faith is also true about relationships, especially Christ-honoring relationships.

In order to persevere through difficult and sometimes debilitating relationships, it must be more like a courtship, a place where we feel safe and respected rather than a courtroom, a place where we feel judged and on trial.

The character, Ninah, from the novel, *The Rapture of Canaan*, by Sheri Reynolds says, "Grudges are bad things. There's only so much room in one heart. You can fill it with love, or you can fill it with resentment. But every bit of resentment you hold takes space away from the love. And the resentment don't do no good no way, but look what love can do."[83]

That is crystal clear discernment.

5

Enthusiasm: "How can I develop redemptively, reconciled relationships?"

ENTHUSIASM: HEART TRAINING FOR ENDURANCE

"None are so old as those who have outlived enthusiasm."[84]

Henry David Thoreau

IT COMES AS a surprise because, well, it is a first. I am sitting in first-class seating on an American Airlines flight out of Orlando, the gift of a crowded flight and a coach-class seating draw.

It is strange. I do not know how to act. However, I quickly notice there is a certain etiquette in first class. Etiquette can be defined as, "given or entitled to preferred treatment and handling."

Being in first-class means acting like you belong there. Holding my ticket stub, I nervously watch every person board. I maintain a "Yes, I do belong in this seat" look on my face. Sitting in only half my seat and wondering what to do with the rest is not the proper posture for the upper crust of frequent flyers and world travelers. Ultimately, I get over it.

Being first-class means acting like you expect to be treated kingly while roosting on your royal throne. It means not being surprised when you get your choice of drink served in a real glass, even before the buckle on your seat belt is snapped. It means not screaming with delight when you discover the meat and rolls with your meal are actually heated separately. It means not bellowing, "You've got to be kidding me," when offered the choice of a red or white wine with your meal. It means not using your pre-dinner, warm washcloth to wash your seating area, but waiting to see the others use it to freshen up their hands and face before the feast. So, I get over it.

While peering out the airplane window into the clouds, I draw an obvious faith parallel to my first-class experience. My first-time encounter with the grace of God was like discovering I had been moved to a first-class window seat next to the pilot when I actually spent all I had on a lower-class coach seat next to roaring engines. Unlike my first-class flying experience, I have never gotten over my first-class grace experience and neither did my father-in-law, Arthur O. Little.

For most of my forty years with him, he always responded to my greeting, "How are you doing?" with two simple words: "First class!" The years of seeing his smile and hearing his life's declaration taught me the sheer power of enthusiasm. The source of the word is the Greek *enthousiasmos*, which ultimately comes from the adjective *entheos*, "having the god within." While definitions differ, the core meaning of enthusiasm is a feeling of energetic interest in a particular subject or activity. An eagerness to be involved is undeniable.[85]

Honestly, I do not know any healthy, vibrant, authentic, vulnerable, and discerning relationships that do not have enthusiasm as a core ingredient. This enthusiasm is not the result of a "fake it 'til you make it" declaration of endurance. This enthusiasm is the result of a life humbled and honed by love and laughter, as well as pain and perspective. This enthusiasm is the fuel that fires the engine of endurance when the weight of yesterday threatens the hope of tomorrow.

Do your relationships have enthusiasm? Have you personally lost your enthusiasm for a relationship and find yourself looking for an exit door? What could you do today to shoot a fresh injection of perspective and enthusiasm, like kindling for a fire, into your flickering relationship?

It was Roy Disney, the elder brother of the famous Walt Disney, who said, "When your values are clear to you, making decisions becomes easier."[86] Values are the principles or standards of behavior that guide our lives. Values are not aspirations. Values are actions because, at the end of the day, behavior trumps ideas every time.

Stay in the Room relationships are not built on nice ideas and wonderful intentions. They are built on desire and performance. They are built on deep-seated values and overwhelming enthusiasm.

Here are five values for "Stay in the Room" relationships that are worthy of our enduring enthusiasm.

I. PRE-EMINENCE OF LOVE VALUE.

The Bible says . . . "Above *all*, keep *fervent* in your love for one another, because love covers a multitude of sins" (I Peter 4: 8).

It is the mid-1990s and I am in a movie theatre listening to a conversation that will linger in my memory for many years. Featuring Forest Gump and his lifetime friend named Jenny, the conversation goes like this:

Forrest: "Will you marry me? I'd make a good husband, Jenny."

Jenny: "You would, Forrest.

Forrest: "But you won't marry me?"

Jenny: "You don't wanna marry me."

Forrest: "Why don't you love me, Jenny? I'm not a smart man.

But I know what love is."[87]

You likely know the movie. It is *Forrest Gump*, the 1994 American epic romantic comedy-drama based on the novel of the same name by Winston Groom. The story depicts life changing events of a naïve and slow-witted, yet athletically gifted, native of Alabama. Forest witnesses and, at times, influences, historically defining moments in the 20th century in the United States. However, it is Forrest's unconditional and enduring love for his childhood sweetheart that brings tears to even the most cynical. For the record, he did know what love is!

Love undergirds all our relationships if we model Christ. Love is a decision to allow anyone access to the relationship room of our lives.

I do not underestimate the difficulty of this room issue. I often call it the proximity premise because the Church of Jesus Christ either lives or dies on this issue: who can gain access or proximity to the heart and favor of God and his people?

Read the Gospels in the New Testament and you will notice Jesus answers the proximity question differently than those around him. He was crucified for it.

Read the book of Acts where again and again, the first-century Church is forced to clarify what a person must do to gain access and proximity to the love and plan of God. Also, in Acts, we witness a major disagreement. You may recognize the story.

Saul of Tarsus (who would later become the Apostle Paul) was a vicious persecutor of Christians. Following his conversion, Christians continued to be afraid of him. A man named Barnabas persuaded the disciples in Jerusalem, to let the apostle fellowship with them (Acts 9:29). As a result of this intercession, a wonderful friendship between Paul and Barnabas formed. They served together faithfully for a season. It is, therefore, sad to note they eventually have a falling out. For some reason, they could not **Stay in the Room** together.

On their first missionary journey, John Mark, the cousin of Barnabas (Colossians 4:10), accompanies them. Along the way, however, John Mark decides to return to his home in Jerusalem (Acts 13:13). The reason for this departure is not specified in the text.

When a second campaign is planned, Barnabas once again proposes taking John Mark as a helper, but Paul resists the idea. The New Testament indicates that a sharp contention develops between them (Acts 15:36-41). They cannot reach an agreement, so they part ways. As far as the record indicates, these two remarkable men never see one another again.

Anyone serious about the Bible and relationships cannot read this story and not be curious. This dissension between Paul and Barnabas does not appear to be over a doctrinal issue. The rupture involves a personal dispute based upon a judgment call. To their credit, neither Paul nor Barnabas let the conflict distract them from their calling.

Someone has suggested an intriguing what-if scenario for the end of our lives. What if we were asked to discern the best and worst of our personal decisions? Chances are we would not remember the purchase of a car or a house, or the promotion we did not receive. The best and worst decisions would likely be when we either failed or succeeded at allowing the pre-eminence of love to rule our lives.

II. TRUTH IN LOVE VALUE.

The Bible says . . . "*Speaking the truth* in love, we are to *grow up* in all aspects into Him, who is the head, even Christ" (Ephesians 4: 15).

We must once again address the granddaddy truth-in-love question of all time: Do we want to be right or redemptive?

That became an important question for me because I am by nature, a confronter. My personality profile tells me I value the truth (or at least my version of it) so much, I will not hesitate to offer my view whenever I am asked and sometimes when I am not.

Not only am I a confronter by nature, but my "nurture" did nothing to deter that tendency. Growing up in a home of screamers, everything we thought was said out loud and most of the time, at a higher than normal decibel level with very colorful language. Imagine my surprise the first time I discussed a frustration with my eventual bride, in what was for me, a normal tone of voice!

If love is not the purifier of our words and attitudes, we are likely to fail in our communication and ultimately dismantle our relationships.

Psychologists have been reminding us of the screamer-sweeper dynamic for years. They say if we conceal our anger, it will lead to depression and if we ventilate our anger it will lead to destruction. So, what we need to do is learn to control it. Oh my, that sounds easy . . . NOT!

So, how do we control ourselves in difficult conversations? A word we often use when talking about control is the word discipline or "the practice of training people to obey rules or a code of behavior."[88]

However, in the spiritual realm, Henri Nouwen offers a fresh perspective to discipline.

While recognizing the control component within psychology, economics and parenting, in the spiritual life the word discipline is defined as "the effort to create some space in which God can act."[89] It means to create room for something unplanned or unexpected to happen.

Let's reflect on my screamer nature that was nurtured by a dysfunctional family. It did not take years of psychology to understand that ventilation of my feelings was hurting more than helping. It also didn't take an anger management course to understand, I was not adequately balancing my need to speak the truth with my willingness to hear the truth.

For years, I spoke of my desire to speak the truth in love, but that didn't become a reality until I began to teach and live out the question: *"Do I want to be right or redemptive?"*

III. NOT EASILY PROVOKED VALUE.

The Bible says "Love is patient, love is kind, and is not jealous; love does not brag and is not arrogant, does not act unbecomingly; it does not seek its own, *is not provoked*, does not take into account a wrong suffered" (I Corinthians 13 4-5).

A simple story will highlight the "not easily provoked" value. An older couple is being interviewed about the longevity of their marriage when the inevitable question is asked: "What would you tell young couples about the success of your marriage and how you were able to stay married so long?"

"Well," the old fellow began, "I would tell them . . . just don't get divorced."

That was a man who knew and practiced with great certainty and valor, the value of not being easily provoked.

Think back over your life and recall the stop signs that ultimately became U-turns. Maybe it was a souring relationship or dead-end job.

Something was said or done that resulted in a turnaround. As you reflect, possibly you were too easily provoked and simply didn't persevere.

A Personal Story of Perseverance

Walking onto the campus of The Southern Baptist Theological Seminary was a dream come true for me. A relatively new believer, the call to full-time ministry was never a doubt. Imagine, I was the little boy who was dressed up for Easter in a clip tie just a few times during childhood and sent down the street to attend a small church. I never knew who Jesus was or anything about truly knowing God until my drinking buddy found God during a youth retreat and thought I should find Him too.

So here I was. I barely knew who Noah or Abraham were, so first year Greek at 8:00 a.m. was a daunting experience! I was determined to conquer the challenge, which I did with all A's.

A Master of Divinity Degree took three years at Southern. Still feeling like a rookie when it came to proficiency in Biblical studies, I felt I should forge ahead. PhD students had to take the GRE and Miller's Analogy tests and getting accepted was highly competitive. I did not realize it at the time, but it was a sort of David and Goliath challenge. I was a street kid, a fighter and survivor of a home where only two of my siblings graduated high school, and none went to college. In a nutshell, analytical thinking and language skills were not emphasized, so standardized tests were not my forte. My GRE score needed to be raised, so I studied unceasingly for a year. The second score was one to be proud of and competitive for acceptance. When I got the letter informing me, I had NOT been accepted into the PhD program, it was devastating. Upon further investigation, I discovered my first and lower score had been reported. Although the powers that be acknowledged their mistake, all slots had been filled. I was informed I would have to do a Master of Theology degree, including writing a thesis of a minimum one hundred pages before reapplying.

After not being easily provoked, I swallowed my pride and went to work. Studies for the additional degree and the thesis took approximately a year. I was rewarded with acceptance into the PhD program. The experience of writing the thesis for the second Masters put me ahead of the game for my PhD dissertation. I completed my degree ahead of some who got in the first time. Perseverance paid off then and continued to throughout my life when there was a river that seemed uncrossable. Most people do not call me Dr. Francis, but I know I am because I earned every bit of it. Perseverance is my friend and every life challenge and relationship demand it.

IV. RAPID RECONCILIATION VALUE.

The Bible says . . . "Be angry, and yet do not sin; do not let the *sun go down* on your anger, and do not give the devil an *opportunity*" (Ephesians 4: 26-27).

While I have learned this verse cannot always be taken literally in terms of the timeframe offered, it is incredibly important. An equally important scripture offers the following admonition: **The Bible** says . . . "If therefore you are presenting your offering at the altar, and there remember that your brother has something against you, leave your offering there before the altar, and go your way; *first be reconciled* to your brother, and then come and present your offering" (Matthew 5: 23-24).

This verse is frightening because it connects our ability to worship with our willingness to be involved in a reconciliation process. Previously mentioned in an earlier chapter, it bears repeating. If we seek reconciliation with the right motive, at the right time, out of obedience to God, he will honor our effort.

The Bible also says . . . "If a fellow believer hurts you, go and tell him—work it out between the two of you" (Matthew 18: 15).

What is at play with these scriptures can be called the "rapid reconciliation" steps:

1. go
2. go privately
3. go with a reconciling spirit

Leonardo da Vinci painted the fresco *The Last Supper* in a church in Milan and stories abound around the mystery and mastery of his experience.

At the time that Leonardo da Vinci painted *The Last Supper*, he had an enemy who was a fellow painter. When da Vinci painted the face of Judas Iscariot, the betrayer of Jesus, he used the face of his enemy so that it would be present for ages as the man who betrayed Jesus. He took delight while painting this picture in knowing that others would notice the face of his enemy on Judas.

As he completed the faces of the other disciples, he then attempted to paint the face of Jesus, but struggled to make any progress. da Vinci felt frustrated and confused. In time he realized what was wrong. His hatred for the other painter was holding him back from finishing the face of Jesus. Only after making peace with his fellow painter and repainting the face of Judas, was he able to paint the face of Jesus and complete his masterpiece.

The "rapid reconciliation" principle is not about time efficiency, like an item to check off the to-do list. It is about soul efficacy. The intended result of God's forgiving us is the direct conduit we have to forgive others.

V. FORGIVE AND FORGE AHEAD VALUE.

The Bible says . . . "Let all bitterness and wrath and anger and clamor and slander *be put away* from you, along with all malice. And be kind to one another, tender-hearted, *forgiving* one another, just as God in Christ also has forgiven you" (Ephesians 4:31-32).

Lewis Smedes' book, *The Art of Forgiveness,* is the Bible on the issue of forgiveness. I have given multiple copies of this book away. He identifies three stages in every act of forgiveness:

1. We **rediscover** the humanity of the person who hurt us.
2. We **surrender** our right to get even.
3. We **revise** our feelings toward the person we forgive.[90]

The Conditions

Smedes distills two hurts that must be answered with the miracle of forgiving. These are acts of disloyalty and betrayal. A disloyal person is a person who treats one like a stranger when they exist as a friend or partner. Disloyalty is serious because it is a violation of trust and history.

Disloyalty evolves into betrayal when it not only makes strangers of people who belong to each other, but makes them enemies. Disloyalty lets people down, but betrayal cuts them into pieces.

The Surgery

Spiritual surgery, the second stage of forgiveness, involves the hurt person's inner response to the one who wronged them. Here the forgiver performs spiritual surgery within his or her own memory and separates the hurt from the person who did the hurting.

The Do Over

The miracle of forgiveness is that two alienated people start over. This Do Over is not perfect. Loose ends are untied, nasty questions are unanswered, and the future is uncertain, but a new start begins. This stage has several qualifiers:

- Forgiving is NOT forgetting.
- Forgiving is NOT excusing.
- Forgiving is NOT smoothing things over.

Smedes powerfully explains this stage:

In the creative violence of love, you reach into the unchangeable past and cut away the wrong from the person who wronged you, you erase the hurt in the archives of your heart. When you pull it off, you do the one thing, the only thing that can remedy the inevitability of painful history. The grace to do it is from God. The decision to do it is our own.[91]

To the guilty, forgiveness is revealed as amazing grace. To the offended, forgiveness sounds like outrageous injustice.

The Fairness of Forgiveness

Simon Wiesenthal was a prisoner in the Mauthausen concentration camp in Poland. One day he was assigned to clean out rubbish from a barn the Germans had improvised into a hospital for wounded soldiers. Toward evening, a nurse took Wiesenthal by the hand and led him to a young SS trooper, his face bandaged with puss-soaked rags, eyes tucked behind the gauze. He was 21 years old.

He grabbed Wiesenthal's hand and clutched it. He said that he had to talk to a Jew; he could not die before he had confessed sins he had committed against helpless Jews, and he had to be forgiven by a Jew before he died. He told Wiesenthal a horrible tale of how his battalion had gunned down Jews, parents, and children who were trying to escape from a house set afire by the SS troopers.

Wiesenthal listened to the dying man's whole story; first the story of his innocent youth, and then the story of his participation in evil. At the end, Wiesenthal jerked his hand away and walked out of the barn: No word was spoken, no forgiveness was given. Wiesenthal would not, could not, forgive. But he was not sure he did the right thing.

He ended his story, "The Sunflower," with a question: "What would you have done?" Thirty-two eminent persons, mostly Jewish, contributed their answers to his hard question. Most said Wiesenthal was right: he should not have forgiven the SS trooper; it would not have been fair. Why should a man who gave his will to the doing of monumental evil expect a quick word of forgiveness on his death-bed? What right had Wiesenthal to forgive the man for evil he had done to other Jews? If Wiesenthal forgave the soldier, he would be saying that the Holocaust was not so evil. "Let the SS trooper go to hell," said one respondent.[92]

At the end of the day, Smedes says, we are only able to overcome the unfairness of forgiveness because we honestly believe that forgiveness is "a better way to fairness."

Forgiveness creates a new possibility of fairness by releasing us from the unfair past. "Forgiving takes us off the escalator of revenge so that both of us can stop the chain of incremented wrongs. We start over. We start over as if the wrongdoer had not hurt us at all. The doorway to justice closes time and time again. Forgiveness remains the only way to open the door."[93]

Forgiveness also brings fairness to the forgiver. It is the hurting person who most feels the burden of unfairness; but he condemns himself to more unfairness if he refuses to forgive.

Ann Lamott says it best: "Not forgiving is like drinking rat poison and then waiting for the rat to die."[94]

How People Forgive

Forgiveness is the most difficult step of all. How do we forgive?

• Forgivers forgive slowly.

C.S. Lewis had a monster for a teacher when he was a boy. He hated that academic sadist most of his life. A few months before his death, he wrote to his American friend: "Dear Mary...Do you know, only a few weeks ago, I realized suddenly that I had at last forgiven the cruel schoolmaster who so darkened my childhood? I had been trying to do it for years."[95] Initially, we cannot; but eventually, we do.

• Forgivers forgive communally.

Forgivers need a crowd because people who hurt and even hate, need persons who struggle as hard as they do to lead the way. Smedes calls it "socialized forgiving."[96]

• Forgivers forgive as they are forgiven

There is not a better example of this truth than Corrie Ten Boom. She was imprisoned during the war years in a concentration camp, humiliated and degraded, especially in the delousing shower where the women were ogled by the leering guards. She made it through that German hell and eventually, she felt she had, by grace, forgiven even those who guarded the shower stalls.

Corrie Ten Boom preached forgiveness for individuals, for all of Europe. She preached it in Bloemendaal, in the United States, and one Sunday, in Munich. After the sermon, greeting people, she saw a man come toward her, hand outstretched: "Ja, Fräulein, it is wonderful that Jesus forgives us all our sins, just as you say."[97]

She remembered his face; his was the leering, lecherous, mocking face of an SS guard of the shower stall. Her hand froze at her side. She could not forgive. She thought she had forgiven all. But she could not forgive when she met the guard, standing in the flesh before her.

Ashamed, horrified at herself, she prayed: "Lord, forgive me, I cannot forgive." As she prayed, she felt forgiven, accepted, in spite of her shabby performance as a famous forgiver.

Her hand was suddenly unfrozen. The ice of hate melted. Her hand went out. She forgave as she felt forgiven and I suspect she would not be able to sort out the difference.

CONCLUSION: A PLEA TO STAY IN THE ROOM

As I write these concluding words, our country has never been more divided. A presidential election takes place tomorrow and it will likely involve more voters going to the ballot box than in over a century. The point is no matter who wins, will we be able to live together? Will we be willing to resolve our differences and **Stay in the Room** together? Or will we give in to our worst instincts and choose being right over being redemptive?

We began this book sharing stories from my journey that seemed impossible and yielded an urge to run. I wanted to run when my dad was electrocuted, my teacher humiliated me, and my stepfather abused me. I wanted to run when my girlfriend was disloyal, a church member predicted my failure, my brother was murdered, and my mother was dying of lung cancer.

When was the last time you wanted to turn and run? Your anticipated run was not a jog from the threat of bodily harm. It was a desperate need to stop the pain of relational misunderstanding and confusion. It was an anxious attempt to thwart the crush of continuing lies and devastating disappointment.

In contrast, when was the last time you wanted to turn around and stay? Your determination to remain in a relationship was not due to resolution of all the personal issues that haunt so many relationships.

Your resolve to "Stay in the Room" with a raw and complex relationship was the result of displaying authenticity, defining boundaries, understanding compatibility, developing discernment and building enthusiasm.

My desire is to paint the possibility that "Staying in the Room" when the temptation to run is powerful, builds personal character and pleases the God who shapes us. May it be so for you.

Endnotes

CHAPTER ONE

1 https://www.quoteambition.com/mark-twain-quotes

2 https://www.youtube.com/watch?v=1sONfxPCTU0

3 Hersey, George L., *The Evolution of Allure: Sexual Selection From the Medici Venus to the Incredible Hulk*, (Cambridge, MIT Press, 1st edition, 1996), pp. 44-59.

4 Balf, Todd, *Outside Magazine*, XXII, Number 2, February, 1997, 40-54.

5 Balf, p. 42.

6 Ibid.

7 https://www.goodreads.com/quotes/865-be-who-you-are-and-say-what-you-feel-because

8 Miller, Keith, *The Secret Life of the Soul*, (B&H Publishing Group, Nashville, Tennessee, 1997), p. 16.

9 "Kentucky man caught at Christian bookstore," *ReligionNewsBlog*, Item 2494, posted February 26, 2003, religionnewsblog.com/00002494.

10 Miller, p. 17.

11 Shafer, Jack, "Dateline: Brooklyn," *The New York Times*, March 14, 2004.

12 Solzhenitsyn, Alexander I., *Cancer Ward*, FSG Classics, p. 432. Farrar, Straus and Giroux. Kindle Edition.

13 Miller, p.24.

14 Grant, Jr., Richard and Miller, Andrea Wells, *Recovering Connections*, (Harper/Collins Publishers, New York, 1992), pp. 10-18.

15 Breen, Bill, *Fast Company*, "Who Do You Love?" December 19, 2007.

16 "Modern solutions for very busy people," *ABC News*, abcnews.go.com.

17 Vargas, Daniel J., "Phony ATM receipts aim to impress women," *Houston Chronicle*, March 5, 2003.

18 Alanez, Tonya, "Fred's Storied Career," *Los Angeles Times*, August 17, 2005; Mankiewicz, Josh. "The ultimate con man." *Dateline NBC transcript*. Aired April 24, 2007.

19 Elsworth, Catherine. "Priest, doctor, fundraiser . . . and con man." *Telegraph. (UK) Web Site*. August 25, 2005.

20 Epstein, Joseph, "Celebrity Culture," *Hedgehog Review,* Spring 2005, Volume Seven, Number One.

21 Geddes, Jennifer I., "An interview with Richard Schickel." *The Hedgehog Review,* volume 7, number 1, 2005, p.82; Also see Richard Schickel, *Intimate Strangers: The Culture of Celebrity,* (Doubleday; New York, 1985).

22 Halpern, Jake, *Fame Junkies,* (Houghton Mifflin Company, Boston, 2007).

23 Lewis, C.S., *The Problem of Pain,* (HarperCollins e-books), p. 91.

24 Umbreit, Kristi, "Woman Runs Marathon by Mistake," *AP News,* May 21, 1990.

25 Kornfield, Jack, *The Art of Forgiveness, Kindness and Peace,* (Bantam Books, New York, 2002), pp.38-39.

26 Breen.

27 Shipnuck, Alan, "Power and Grace," *Sports Illustrated,* April 16, 2012.

28 "How Bobby Petrino games system by hiring mistress Jessica Dorrell," *Sports Illustrated,* April 13, 2012.

29 Ibid.

30 Williams, Margery, *The Velveteen Rabbit,* (Doubleday & Company, Inc, New York, digital library).

CHAPTER TWO

31 https://www.brainyquote.com/quotes/edwin_louis_cole_360078

32 https://www.goodreads.com/quotes/24553-no-is-a-complete-sentence

33 Cloud, Henry and Townsend, John, *Boundaries,* (Zondervan Publishing House, Grand Rapids, 1992), p. 27.

34 Ibid, p. 28.

35 Whitfield, Charles L., *Boundaries and Relationships: Knowing, Protecting and Enjoying the Self,* (Kindle Edition).

36 Whitfield, Location 707.

37 Whitfield, Location 710.

38 Whitfield, Location 713-14

39 https://storyofsong.com/story/you-cant-always-get-want/

40 Linden, Anne, *Boundaries in Human Relationships: How to Be Separate and Connected,* (Crown House Publishing, United Kingdom, 2008), pp. 44-45.

41 Cloud and Townsend, p. 29.

42 Cloud and Townsend, p. 32.

43 Cloud and Townsend, p. 34.

44 Cloud and Townsend, p. 100.

45 Cloud and Townsend, p. 102.

46 Ben-Zeev, Aaron, "Why We All Need to Belong to Someone," *Psychology Today,* March 11, 2014.

47 "The ultimate value of life depends upon awareness rather than mere survival," *The Lafourche Gazette,* June 23, 2017.

48 Goldman, Daniel, *Emotional Intelligence,* (Bantam Books, New York, 1995, (p. 43).

49 Ibid, p. 48.

50 Cloud and Townsend, p. 103.

51 Craddock, *Fred Craddock Stories,* (Chalice Press, St. Louis, Missouri, 2001) pp 60-61.

CHAPTER THREE

52 https://www.brainyquote.com/quotes/stevie_nicks_189415

53 Lewis, C.S., *Mere Christianity,* (The Macmillan Company, New York, 1967), p. 182.

54 https://tweakingo.com/thomas-a-kempis-quotes-and-short-biography/

55 http://www.quotationspage.com/quote/11872.html

56 https://gestalttheory.com/fritzperls/gestalttherapy/

57 https://www.azlyrics.com/lyrics/beyonceknowles/memyselfi.html

58 https://loveishopeful.wordpress.com/2012/02/07/meaningful-quote-beyond-perls/

59 https://www.goodreads.com/quotes/965694-most-people-when-directly-confronted-by-evidence-that-they-are

60 https://www.azquotes.com/author/23761-George_Arthur_Buttrick

61 https://www.azquotes.com/quote/804906

62 https://www.facebook.com/ransomedheartministries/posts/10154864087194240

63 Swift, W. M., "Mystery at Sea," *Sports Illustrated,* November 30, 1992; also see Julia Plant, *Coyote Lost at Sea,* (International Marine/McGraw-Hill Foundation, New York, 2013).

64 https://www.yourdictionary.com/reconciliation

65 Larson, Keith, *A Hunger for Healing*, (HarperCollins, New York, 1991), pp. 132-133.

CHAPTER FOUR

66 https://www.goodreads.com/quotes/3749-you-can-get-all-a-s-and-still-flunk-life

67 https://www.dictionary.com/browse/discern

68 https://quotecatalog.com/quote/tonya-hurley-if-you-expect-n-KpYZWma

69 https://www.goodreads.com/quotes/422993-treat-a-man-as-he-is-and-he-will-remain

70 "No More Gym? Don't Worry, Your Muscles Remember," *NPR*, August 22, 2010.

71 Synder, C.R., *The Psychology of Hope*, (Simon & Schuster, Inc., New York, 1994), p. 8.

72 Burns, John F., "Millvina Dean, Titanic's Last Survivor," *New York Times*, May 31, 2009.

73 https://www.brainyquote.com/authors/antisthenes-quotes

74 Rosenburg, Michael, "The Marine and the Orphan," p. 82-84, *Sports Illustrated*, August 27, 2012.

75 https://www.merriam-webster.com/dictionary/collaborate

76 https://www.merriam-webster.com/dictionary/trust

77 https://www.azquotes.com/quote/1360988

78 Brown, Brené, *Rising Strong: How the Ability to Reset Transforms the Way We Live, Love, Parent, and Lead*, (Random House Publishing Group, Kindle Edition), Location 2783/4060.

79 Ibid.

80 http://www.georgemacdonaldquotes.com/to-be-trusted/tobetrusted/

81 Wines, Michael, "'None of Us Can Get Out' Kursk Sailor Wrote," *New York Times*, October 27, 2000.

82 As cited in Erdahl, Lowell O., *Joyful Living*, (CSS Publishing Company, Inc., Lima, Ohio, 2002), p. 29.

83 Sheri Reynolds, *The Rapture of Canaan*, (New York: Penguin Group, 1995), pp. 291-292.

CHAPTER FIVE

84 www.brainyquote.com/quotes/henry_david_thoreau_103923

85 https://dictionary.cambridge.org/us/dictionary/english/enthusiasm

86 Colan, Lee, "A Lesson from Roy A. Disney on Making Values-based Decisions," *Inc.*, July 24, 2019.

87 https://everydaypower.com/forrest-gump-quotes/

88 https://www.oxfordreference.com/view/10.1093/oi/authority. 20110803095721587

89 https://lifeondoverbeach.wordpress.com/2010/08/06/henri-nouwen-on-the-spiritual-disciplines/

90 Smedes, Lewis, *The Art of Forgiveness*, (The Random House Publishing Group, New York, 1996), pp. 5-6.

91 Smedes, Lewis, "Forgiveness—The Power to Change the Past," *Christianity Today*, December 1, 2002.

92 Smedes.

93 Smedes.

94 Lamott, Ann, *Traveling Mercies: Some Thoughts on Faith*, (New York: Random House, 1999), p.134.

95 C.S. Lewis, *Collected Letters, Vol. III*, Narnia, Cambridge and Joy, 1950-1963, edited by Walter Hooper, (HarperCollins London, 2006), p. 1438.

96 Smedes.

97 http://www.fatherpius.site/enjoy-the-freedom-of-god/reflections/the-insanity-of-forgiveness/